The Science of Settlement
Ideas for Negotiators

American Law Institute
American Bar Association
Continuing Professional Education

ALI ABA

American Law Institute | American Bar Association

Continuing Leadership in Professional Education

The Science of Settlement
Ideas for Negotiators

Barry Goldman, MA, JD

ALI ABA
American Law Institute | American Bar Association
Continuing Leadership in Professional Education

4025 Chestnut Street | Philadelphia, Pennsylvania 19104-2899 | www.ali-aba.org

Library of Congress Control Number: 2008922665

Printed in the United States of America

Fourth Printing 2008

ISBN: 978-0-8318-0011-6

John B. Spitzer of the ALI-ABA staff
supervised the production of this book.

ALI-ABA has a history of outreach to underrepresented groups in the legal community and is firmly committed to providing a welcoming environment and ensuring that the attorneys who speak and write for our organization represent the increasing diversity of our profession. We welcome suggestions for new speakers and authors, especially from underrepresented groups in the legal community, to support the full participation of all of the talent in our profession.

Acknowledgements

This book has many parents. Stuart Israel and Doug Van Epps fostered the idea and steered me to ALI-ABA. Mark Carroll read the first draft and left the most inspiring voicemail message I've ever received. John Spitzer shepherded the project through the publishing process. Joe Danowsky, my editor and now my friend, pored over every line and challenged my thinking as well as my writing. Both have benefited immensely from his efforts.

Baruch Fischhoff, Bob Creo and Doug Yarn kindly read drafts and made valuable suggestions. Ben Koss and Irv Margulies found mistakes and made encouraging noises. Amy Koss spent far too many hours on the phone with me talking about writing when we both should have been working. Mike Rosen has been helping me think since we were children. Working with the incomparable Katie Maratta has been pure joy.

My parents, Max and Harriet Goldman, have always been an inspiration. I hope this brings them *naches*.

The time and attention it took to write this book had to come from somewhere. In a very real sense, I stole them from my wife. I look forward to paying her back.

B.G.

Dedication

For Susan, my *ezer k'negdo*

We don't see things as they are, we see them as we are.

— Anais Nin

Figures

1. Outcome of Trusting or Fearing a Stranger **58**

2. Zone of Possible Agreement ("ZOPA") **74**

3. Pareto-Optimal Frontier **148**

Contents

Chapter 1	**Introduction**	**1**
1.01	The Ultimatum Game	**3**
1.02	Monkey Justice?	**6**
1.03	Disclaimers And Caveats	**7**
Chapter 2	**Preparation**	**9**
2.01	Evaluating Your Case	**13**
	(a) The Lake Wobegon Effect	**14**
	(b) Base Rates	**15**
	(c) Overconfidence	**16**
	(d) Self-Serving Bias	**19**
	(e) Endowment Effect	**21**
	(f) Illusion Of Control	**24**
	(g) Belief In A Just World	**26**
	(h) Fundamental Attribution Error	**26**
	(i) Availability Heuristic	**27**
	(j) Probability	**29**
	(k) The Conjunction Fallacy	**30**
	(l) Status Quo Bias	**31**
	(m) Regret Aversion	**33**
	(n) How To Deal With 2.01(a)-(m)	**33**
2.02	The Setup	**36**
	(a) Style	**43**
	(b) Plan Of Concessions	**46**
	(c) Stickiness	**48**
	(d) The Contrast Effect	**50**
2.03	The Schmooze	**53**
	(a) Liking	**55**
	(b) Similarity-Attraction Effect	**57**
	(c) Authority	**60**
	(d) Food	**61**
	(e) Listening	**64**
	(f) Being Observed To Be Listening	**65**

Chapter 3	**Bargaining**	**67**
3.01	The First Offer	**67**
	(a) Anchoring	**67**
	(b) The Winner's Curse	**70**
3.02	Responses To The First Offer	**72**
	(a) The ZOPA	**73**
	(b) Alternative First Response: A Cheap Trick	**75**
3.03	Bargaining Confounds	**76**
	(a) Reciprocity	**76**
	(b) The Prisoner's Dilemma	**79**
	(c) Rejection Then Retreat	**85**
	(d) More Packaging Effects	**85**
	(e) Choices	**88**
	(f) Reactive Devaluation	**92**
	(g) Finding What We Are Looking For	**97**
	(h) Loss Aversion And Framing Effects	**98**
	(i) Size And Timing Of Concessions	**104**
	(j) Scarcity	**106**
	(k) Commitment And Consistency	**108**
	(l) Confirmation Bias	**113**
	(m) Theory Of Mind	**117**
	(n) Partisan Perception	**118**
	(o) Social Proof	**120**
	(p) Sunk Costs	**123**
	(q) Escalation Of Commitment	**126**
	(r) Biased Punctuation Of Conflict	**127**
	(s) Conversational Style	**128**
	(t) Mental Accounting	**129**
	(u) Timing Effects	**131**
	(v) Position Effects	**133**
	(w) Certainty Effect	**134**
	(x) Priming And Schemas	**136**
3.04	Why Mediation Works	**140**
Chapter 4	**Agreements**	**143**
4.01	Counterfactuals	**148**
4.02	The Peak-End Rule	**150**
4.03	Post-Settlement Settlement	**151**
4.04	Gloating	**153**
4.05	A Warning	**153**

Chapter 5 Experiments **155**
5.01 The Lawsuit Market **156**
5.02 The Spinner In The Pie: An Evaluation Tool **157**
5.03 The Lawsuit Market Meets The Spinner In The Pie **160**
5.04 The Lawsuit Market And The Spinner Meet The Status Quo Bias **160**
Chapter 6 Epilogue: Gaming The System IS The System **163**
Glossary **169**
Bibliography **179**
Index **189**

1

Introduction

Everyone knows the story about the five blind men and the elephant. Each man touches a different part of the elephant and comes up with a different description of what an elephant is like. Less well known is the story of the five blind elephants who were asked to describe a man. They were unanimous. "Man is flat," they said.

The story illustrates the fact that the tools we use to investigate the world determine how the world is perceived. The tools human beings use to investigate the world are our senses and our brains. The senses give us information about what is out there in the world. The brain processes that information, along with the information it already has about our goals and so on, and tells us what to do. The eyes tell the brain there is food over there. The brain says "Food is good. Let's go over there." And we go over there. Simple. But incomplete.

First, the senses don't always give us accurate information. Second, the information processing system itself has limits. The most familiar examples of these inaccuracies and limitations are optical illusions. This book is about an analogous phenomenon called cognitive illusions.

As negotiators and mediators have always known, and as economists and cognitive scientists are coming to understand, human beings do not process information and make decisions according to the rules of reason and logic. Instead, we make decisions based on rules of thumb, mental shortcuts called "heuristics." This is so for two reasons. First, humans have never had enough time or energy to think carefully about every decision we have to make. We need decision-making strategies that we can apply quickly and without much mental effort to the majority of our decisions.

Second, trade-offs have to be made in the design of any system. You could build a car that's perfectly safe, but it would be too heavy to drive. You could build a word-processing program or a cell phone with hundreds or thousands of clever features, but it would be too complicated to use. In designing a decision-making system, there have to be trade-offs between speed and accuracy and between accuracy and cost. Over the millennia, evolution made those design choices based on natural selection. Organisms that had the optimal ratios between speed, accuracy and cost had a reproductive advantage and produced more offspring.

Like any system, though, our information processing and decision-making systems have limitations. There are circumstances when the heuristics don't work, when they produce bad answers.

Partly, this is because the environment we lived in when the heuristics were wired into how we think — generally considered to be the African Savanna during the Pleistocene — is not the environment we now inhabit. Strategies that were adaptive in the ancestral environment, design features that were optimal for solving the problems presented by that environment, are likely not to be adaptive anymore.

The easiest way to see this is to consider the heuristic *Always Eat As Much As You Can.* In the ancestral environment, *Always Eat As*

Much As You Can was a good idea, an adaptive strategy. Populations that used the heuristic were able to survive periods of food scarcity better than populations that didn't. In suburban America in the 21st Century, when there is a fast-food restaurant on every corner, *Always Eat As Much As You Can* is not an adaptive strategy. But it is so deeply wired that many of us have difficulty resisting it, with obvious consequences.

Recent work by psychologists and economists has uncovered a great number of biases, heuristics and cognitive illusions at work in the way we process information and make decisions, and evolutionary psychologists have formulated theories to explain why these heuristics were originally adaptive. We will touch on some of that theorizing, but it will not be our major focus. What we care about as negotiators is identifying the heuristics that are at work in the minds of our clients, our opponents and ourselves as we formulate and evaluate negotiation positions. If we can identify the rules being used to process information, we can predict the decisions that will result. To the extent we can frame the presentation of information so that it triggers the use of preferred heuristics, we can influence those decisions.

In other words, the goal of this book is to identify the biases, heuristics and cognitive illusions that affect decision making in negotiation. With that knowledge, we hope to prepare ourselves to work with the natural wiring of the brain rather than against it in formulating negotiating positions. If it works, this ought to increase the likelihood our proposals will be accepted and reduce the likelihood that the packaging of an unfavorable proposal will persuade us to accept a settlement we should not.

§1.01 THE ULTIMATUM GAME

Suppose you are sitting in a bar. Sitting next to you is a perfect stranger. Another person you've never seen before walks in and, addressing the two of you, makes the following offer. He says "I have here $20 in dollar bills. I am going to hand these bills to one of you and ask you to divide them with the person sitting next to you. You can divide them any way you want. The person receiving the bills will then be allowed either to accept the split you propose or reject it. If he accepts, you both keep the money as divided. If he rejects, I take all the money back." What would you do? What would you offer if you were the offeror and what would you accept if you were the offeree? Don't read the next paragraph until you have decided.

* * *

What rules, what heuristics, did you use to make this determination? One answer might be that we make the decision that will net us the greatest number of dollars. This is the traditional view. Given two choices, always choose the one with the greatest net dollar benefit to me.

If we try to predict the results of this experiment using that heuristic, the answer is that the offeror would give the smallest increment available and the receiver would accept it. This is straight out of utility maximization theory. The offeree reasons thus: One dollar (or one penny!) is better than nothing. My choices are to accept the offer of one dollar and get a dollar, or reject it and get nothing. Since a dollar is better than nothing and those are my only choices, I'll take it.

The offeror's reasoning is the same. My goal is to maximize my utility. My utility is maximized if I get all the money. But the offeree will reject if I offer him nothing. So I will offer him the smallest increment allowed. That provides the maximum for me and assures that the offeree will not reject. Offer a dollar.

This reasoning uses the ***Homo economicus*** model. According to this model, the economic man will always seek to maximize his utility. He will behave according to a rational analysis of his best interests. If he fails to do so it must be because of a lack of information or a mistake in information processing.

It turns out, however, if you actually do the experiment, that people rarely offer one another lopsided deals, and when they do they are almost always rejected. What people offer is closer to a 50/50 split. *Homo economicus* theory is wrong. People will regularly punish themselves — take nothing rather than something — in order to *teach a lesson* to the ungenerous. And offerors know it. This does not make sense according to classical economic theory, but the result is quite robust. A new theory is needed (Shell, 1999, p. 62).

Douglas Yarn and Gregory Todd Jones at Georgia State say, "As behavioral negotiation theory has begun to mature, *Homo economicus* has begun to evolve into *homo sapiens.*" (Yarn & Jones, p. 288).

Actually, what is happening as a result of the research in this area is the reemergence of an old theory: the idea that we have a rational mind and an emotional one. George Loewenstein at Carnegie Mellon said, "The new science of neuro-economics is lending support to a very ancient view of human behavior. That is the idea that there is a conflict and interaction between passion, and reason and self-interest" (quoted in Henderson, 2006). The evolutionarily older, more primitive, emotional part of the brain, the limbic system, wants to take the small offer. But the rational part of the brain, the cortex, won't have it. The reaction that says "Screw you and your crummy offer" is an important part of what makes us human.

Daniel Kahneman, along with the late Amos Tversky, is the father of the study of heuristics and biases. Following Stanovich and West (2000), he calls the two parts of the mind **System 1** and **System 2**. In his 2002 Nobel Lecture, Kahneman said: "The operations of System 1 are fast, automatic, effortless, associative, and difficult to control or modify. The operations of System 2 are slower, serial, effortful, and deliberately controlled; they are also relatively flexible and potentially ruled-governed" (Kahneman, 2002). According to Kahneman, "We run mostly on System 1 software" (quoted in Zweig, 2007, p. 14).

I am oversimplifying, of course. The ultimatum game and its relatives have been the subject of extensive academic interest. There are shelves of careful studies on the subject. But for our purposes the point is only this: It ain't only the money. People care about things other than money. For good, evolutionary reasons, we care about fairness.

A negotiator who proceeds as though it's all about the money is missing an important feature of human judgment. And a negotiator whose analysis is missing an important feature of human judgment is not doing himself or his clients any favors.

§1.02 MONKEY JUSTICE?

This concern with fairness is not a recent phenomenon. Monkeys seem to care about it too. An experiment by Sara Brosnan and Frans de Waal at the Yerkes primate observatory near Atlanta makes the point. Brosnan placed two capuchin monkeys in cages where each could see what was happening to the other. She taught the monkeys to complete a simple task and get a reward. Brosnan would hand the monkey a small token, and the monkey was supposed to hand it back. If the monkey completed the task, it got a food reward. There were two types of reward, cucumber slices and grapes. The monkeys will do the task for either reward, but they like grapes better.

Working with monkey number one, Brosnan hands him a token. Monkey hands it back and Brosnan gives him a grape. Brosnan hands him another token. He hands it back and Brosnan gives him another grape. She does this a few more times with monkey number two watching intently. Finally, it's monkey two's turn. Brosnan hands him a token. He hands it back. She gives him a cucumber.

Classical theory predicts that a hungry monkey presented with a desirable food item will take it and eat it. It doesn't make sense looking at the experiment with our familiar theory of utility maximization to expect any other result. Even if we think in evolutionary terms, a monkey who does not always eat as much as he can does not appear to be well adapted to an environment in which food scarcity is likely to be a problem. But that isn't what happens.

In one video of the experiment, the monkey throws the cucumber on the floor of the cage, retreats to a corner and sulks. Monkey number one reaches through the bars, retrieves the cucumber and gobbles it happily.

A monkey will decline food and refuse to participate in an experiment if he thinks he isn't being treated fairly. A monkey.

So what? What does the behavior of captive monkeys and the subjects of social psychology experiments have to do with becoming a more effective negotiator?

First, as an old friend of mine used to say, "Folks is critters." It is a mistake to try to predict how humans will behave using a theory that only includes the highest-level, most recently acquired kinds of cognitive functioning. A full-blooded theory of human behavior will include the characteristics we inherited from our primate ancestors as well. Second, a predictive theory of human interactions is going to include the biases and heuristics our species has acquired over the millennia.

Is this glib? Yes. There are a lot of garbage explanations that begin: Well, you see, in the Pleistocene... reproductive success required.... Critics call these Just So Stories, and no doubt the critics are correct. It's like the record *How to Speak Hip* from the early '60s (www.howtospeakhip.com): Learn to say "like," "dig" and "man" in every sentence, and the rest is easy. Here it's reproductive success, adaptation and evolutionary pressure. But just because some evolutionary psychology is foolishness doesn't mean it all is. Besides, for purposes of becoming a better negotiator we don't need a full-blown theory.

It's like designing a billboard to catch the attention of passing motorists. I don't need a complete theory about visual perception. All I need are some rules about what colors show up best and what images stay in memory. If I know that and the other billboard designers don't, my clients sell more soap.

If we know how the brain works, how it evaluates options, how it formulates choices, how it processes information and makes judgments, we can make predictions and influence results.

One way to do this is anecdotally. We can become more effective negotiators by the seat of our pants. There are plenty of good negotiators who have a bag of tricks and a feel for when to use which one. Or we can do it systematically. The field of dispute resolution already has a sufficient supply of anecdote and hocus pocus, but precious little science. If the field is ever to take its place as a genuine area of knowledge, that ratio is going to have to change.

§1.03 DISCLAIMERS AND CAVEATS

Having just said that we need a better scientific grounding for the field of Dispute Resolution, I should confess that I am not a scientist. I'm not a psychologist or an economist or a cognitive scientist or a primatologist or any of the other kinds of specialists who have contributed to the modern understanding of how human beings make decisions. I don't read the primary literature in any of these fields, and I recognize that my discussion of these ideas lacks the subtlety and nuance we would find in the scientific literature. Still, I think my basic understanding is good enough for what I'm trying to do. As a Dispute Resolution practitioner, the problems I am asked to solve involve particular litigants in particular cases. I am interested in the theory of judgment and decision making because I want to become a more effective practitioner.

* * *

The careful reader will have noticed that we are only a small number of pages into this book, and I already contradicted myself. I gave *Always Eat As Much As You Can* as an example of a heuristic at work in our decision making; then I pointed out an example of monkeys behaving contrary to the way the heuristic would predict. We are going to have to get used to this. Humans are complicated. Our behavior is the combination of many factors. Sometimes different heuristics act in different directions, and the results are difficult to predict. That doesn't mean the task is hopeless or that the project of understanding negotiation behavior through a study of cognitive heuristics will yield a system like astrology or psychoanalysis, where any result can be confidently predicted from any condition (after the fact). It just makes the project more interesting.

2

Preparation

Negotiating a deal is like painting a room. It's all about the prep. The part where you put the paint on the walls is easy. It's the scraping and sanding and taping that take the time and effort.

Negotiating without preparation — trusting your instincts or "going with the flow" — is a dreadful mistake. But just what is it you are supposed to prepare?

Obviously you need to know your file. As the former NPR radio personality John Hockenberry once said, "The best way to sound like you know what you're talking about is to know what you're talking about." Even a negotiation book as helpful as this one is not going to overcome that brutal fact of life.

Obviously it is in your interest to gain as much market knowledge as you can and to learn as much as possible about your negotiation opponent and the circumstances of your negotiation. If you are selling axolotls you need to know about the axolotl market in general and about your axolotl buyer in particular. Not just his position in the axolotl market, his current need for axolotls, and so on, but also his negotiating style.

You need to know your bottom line, the price at which you will walk away. This is usually called your **reservation point** in the negotiation literature. It is named after the auctioneer's practice of setting a reserve price below which an auctioned item will not be sold.

Your reservation price, in turn, is based on your **BATNA** — your best alternative to a negotiated agreement. If you have read any other books on negotiation written in the past 20 years, you probably know that Roger Fisher and William Ury coined that term in their famous 1983 book *Getting To Yes.*

Knowing your BATNA, the best deal you could get elsewhere, is key to evaluating the deal on the table. If you don't know your BATNA you are flying blind and you are likely to get your pocket picked. Worse, you are likely never to know you were robbed. If your opponent is skillful he will make you feel that you got a terrific deal so you will cheerfully return another time to let yourself be robbed again.

You can strengthen your negotiating leverage by improving your BATNA. If you are negotiating for a raise, the most effective way you can improve your leverage is to get another job offer at an increased salary elsewhere. Come back to the table with that job offer in your pocket, and your negotiating position has improved dramatically. If your opponent can beat your BATNA, take the deal on the table. If not, take the BATNA deal and you're still ahead of the status quo.

Notice that this important work takes place away from the table, with a party other than your negotiation opponent. Often negotiators concentrate so much on the deal in front of them that they forget what they might accomplish by pulling back to look at the larger context. You improve your leverage at the negotiating table by improving your alternative away from the table, your BATNA.

Ury and Fisher are right about BATNA: It would be foolish to enter a significant negotiation without having researched it carefully and improved it where possible. But it is not the most important concept in determining optimum negotiation outcomes. That concept is your **aspiration point** — your high-end goal.

The problem with concentrating on your BATNA is that when you reach it, you relax. If your mind is fixed on the point at which you exceed the status quo, the tendency is to stop. But the negotiator who stops negotiating may never learn that there was significantly more potential gain in the deal if he had kept looking for it. This is leaving money on the table, and it is bad.

The trick is to devote your mental energy to pursuing your maximum potential outcome, not your minimally acceptable one — your aspiration point, not your BATNA. People who set high goals achieve better results than people who set low goals. It's just a fact.

* * *

This might be a good time to talk about Happiness and the Meaning of Life. It will only take a moment. If you are getting what you set out to get in most of your negotiations, you are probably leaving money on the table. You could have done better; that is, you could have gotten more stuff if you had bargained harder. From a purely *Homo economicus* point of view, the prescription for that condition is to raise your aspiration points. Ask for more. You won't always get what you ask for, but you will get more if you ask for more. High outcomes correlate with high aspiration points.

Note, however, this is the opposite of the advice you would get from, say, the Buddha about how to achieve happiness. That can be achieved, Buddha taught us, only by wanting less, by lowering our aspiration points. The desire for things cannot be satisfied with things. The desire for things is like a fire. The more things you feed it, the bigger it grows.

"Who is rich?" the *Talmud* asks. "He who is satisfied with what he has." (*Ethics of the Fathers* 4:1.)

This is a book about negotiation and about using psychology to get more stuff. I don't want anybody coming back to me complaining that they got more stuff but it didn't make them happy. That's another book.

* * *

So, you want to prepare for your negotiation by doing the usual homework, by increasing your market knowledge, by improving your BATNA, and by developing a high aspiration point.

One way to get your aspiration point burned into your thinking is to write it down. This sounds like superstition, but the evidence is that it works. There is something about the act of writing that commits us to our goals more strongly than the same goal held by the same person but not written down. There is even evidence that the process is neurological, that the process of writing something down has an observable physical effect on the brain. The literature suggests that after writing down your aspiration point you should carry it with you and take it out to look at periodically during negotiations.

You are supposed to do this at auctions too. Write down the maximum you will pay for an object before the bidding starts, and do not let the excitement of bidding change your mind.

You can see why this makes sense. Before the auction starts you are calm and dispassionate. You want that Louis Philippe commode, and you have a rational idea of what you are willing to spend to get it. An hour later when the bidding starts you are still you and the commode is still the commode, but you find you want it more than you thought and you are willing to raise your bid. Why?

Because auctions are exciting, and when we are excited we think less clearly. Auctions are designed precisely to generate this effect. You bid and the commode is yours. Then someone else bids and the commode is not yours. That bastard took my commode! You bid again and the process repeats. The feeling of loss is completely manufactured by the auction process itself but, as we shall see in §3.03(h), manufactured or not, the feeling of loss is a powerful motivator.

Think about the conversation you are likely to have with yourself as an auction or negotiation proceeds. The excited side of you says, "We need to re-evaluate and raise our maximum bid." The prudent side of you reminds the excited side that this is what we anticipated and it is precisely why we settled on a maximum bid. The excited side says, "But things have changed!" It is at this point that the rational side must ask, "What things, exactly, have changed?"

The excited side can have no answer. Nothing has changed *with respect to the deal.* The only change has been in the emotional context of the deal. And you are not buying an emotional context. You are buying a commode.

Note that this is different from other occasions when it may be appropriate to re-evaluate your earlier commitments. The great strategic thinker and Nobel Prize winner Thomas Schelling tells a story about himself as a youngster that makes the point. The young Schelling decided he wanted to be a polar explorer. To prepare himself for his adventures, he determined to sleep without a blanket.

It was a warm boy who made the decision to sleep without a blanket. But it was a cold boy who had to decide whether to follow through (Shelling, 1984, p. 58). In that case there was a meaningful difference between planning and execution. There was important new information about the deal. What was previously an abstract idea became a physical reality. The warm boy did not understand what he was committing to. In the case of the auction, however, there is no change in physical reality and no new information about the deal. There is only a change in emotional context.

I don't deny that the pull of emotions is strong, or that a change in emotional context *feels* like a change in physical reality. But when the prudent negotiator gets the feeling that things have changed, he tries to remember to ask himself what has changed. He pauses to isolate changes in emotional context from changes in objectively relevant information. One way to bind yourself to the mast so you don't get swept away by emotional context is to carry a written copy of your previous, well-reasoned goal and to look at it from time to time. Your planning is pointless if you ignore it.

§2.01 EVALUATING YOUR CASE

Having just argued that you should set a high aspiration point and keep it actively in mind, now I want to emphasize the opposite. (I said this would happen.) It is equally necessary to keep your expectations under control.

Several psychological features tend to pull our valuations upward into unrealistic territory. We need to understand them and adjust for them.

First, we need to spend a few minutes talking about your attitude.

§2.01(a) The Lake Wobegon Effect

"About 80 percent of us believe that our driving skills are better than average.... [A] large majority of people believe themselves to be smarter, more attractive, and more talented than average..." (Kahneman & Renshon, 2007).

"In one study, 94% of men ranked themselves in the top half of male athletic ability" (Burnham & Phelan, 2000, p. 91).

In a lovely book called *Don't Believe Everything You Think*, Thomas Kida (2006) cites a study of a million high school seniors. Seventy percent regarded themselves as above average in leadership ability, with only 2 percent rating themselves below average. *All* the students thought they were above average in their ability to get along with others. In fact, 25 percent of the students believed their skill in getting along with others was in the top 1 percent. Ninety-four percent of college professors in another study believed they were better than the average professor. (p. 109)

This tendency to exaggerate our virtues and abilities relative to others is called the **Lake Wobegon effect**, after the little town made famous by Garrison Keillor. In Lake Wobegon "All the women are strong, all the men are good-looking, and all the children are above average."

It appears we are so taken with this impossible state of affairs that the contrary frightens us. An apocryphal story has it that former President Dwight Eisenhower "was appalled to learn that about half of our children had below average intelligence, thinking that something had to be done about such poor performance" (Kida, 2006, p. 17).

We don't tend to think we are better than average in areas where actual measurement is possible, free-throw shooting for example. But if the criteria are sufficiently fuzzy, most of us give ourselves the benefit of the doubt. "People believe that, on average, they are more honest, capable, intelligent, courteous, insightful and fair than others" (Bazerman & Neale, 1992, p. 61).

Thomas Schelling explains how it's done. We can all believe we are better than average drivers because:

[E]verybody ranks himself high in qualities he values:

> Careful drivers give weight to care, skillful drivers give weight to skill, and those who think that, what ever else they are not, at least they are polite, give weight to courtesy, and come out high on their own scale. This is the way that every child has the best dog on the block. (Quoted in Gilovich, 1991, p. 84)

Our susceptibility to the Lake Wobegon effect is one of the psychological factors that tend to skew our case evaluations upward.

§2.01(b) Base Rates

It is also true that we do not see our own situation as related to the **base rate**. If we ask a roomful of randomly chosen people how many of them believe they will die of heart disease or get divorced, almost no hands go up. If we ask a roomful of new business owners how many of them will succeed, we get unanimity. The base rates, of course, tell a different story. Many of us will die of heart disease, half of all marriages end in divorce, and most new businesses fail.

Here's another approach to the same problem. Respondents were given this description of a 30-year-old American named Steve: "very shy and withdrawn, invariably helpful but with little real interest in people or the social world. A meek and tidy soul, he has a need for order and structure and a passion for detail." Respondents were then asked if they thought Steve was more likely to work as a farmer or as a librarian.

Steve, of course, neatly fits the profile of the stereotypical librarian and he's far from the stereotype of a farmer. So most people commit what is known as the **representativeness fallacy** and assume he's more likely to be a librarian. The problem with this analysis is that it ignores the base rate. America has many times more farmers than librarians (at least 100:1 by Piatelli-Palmarini's estimate, p. 74). We all know that, but few of us even consider how that fact might affect our answer. We ignore base rates. It is another example of the way we make decisions based on simple heuristics and not on evidence from the real world.

§2.01(c) Overconfidence

Evolutionary psychology suggests that one reason we ignore the base rate with respect to our own success is that confidence is sexy; people who appear confident have more mating opportunities and therefore more reproductive success. In a sense we have been selectively bred for overconfidence. Consequently, I am convinced that I'm successful. If I make a lot of money, I define success in terms of money. If I don't make much money but I get a lot of requests for pro bono speaking engagements, I define success in terms of public respect. If I have neither money nor respect, I define it in terms of the satisfaction I get from my garden or my grandchildren or my collection of Hummel figurines. And if I have none of the above, I define success in terms of my knowledge that there is a place prepared for me in heaven. Not for me the fleeting pleasures of this world. I lay my treasures up "where neither moth nor rust doth corrupt" (*Matthew* 6:20). However it is reached, the conclusion is foregone. I am doing fine.

There is some evidence that the only people who have a realistic view of their true talents and true likelihood of success are the clinically depressed (Fine, 2006, p. 23).

Here's a classic test of overconfidence. Ten questions appear below. Your goal is to supply an answer to each question in the form of a range. Select a range so that you have 90 percent confidence that the true answer to each question lies within the range you selected. Since there are 10 questions and you are answering each with a confidence of 90 percent, you will have done perfectly on the test if you get 9 correct.

1. Martin Luther King's age at death
2. Length of the Nile River
3. Number of countries that are members of OPEC
4. Number of books in the Old Testament
5. Diameter of the moon
6. Weight of an empty Boeing 747
7. Year in which Wolfgang Amadeus Mozart was born

8. Gestation period (in days) of an Asian elephant
9. Air distance from London to Tokyo
10. Deepest known point in the oceans.

(Russo & Schoemaker, 1990/1989, p. 71)

Answers appear at: www.ali-aba.org/BK43/

Most people are wildly inaccurate in this kind of test, but they are not randomly inaccurate. If people were just no good at judging how confident they should be in their estimates, we would see as much under-confidence as overconfidence. But that is not what the test shows. Overwhelmingly it shows overconfidence, in experiment after experiment. It would be a mistake to suppose that this is just some harmless anomaly having to do with judgments of confidence in trivia answers. The test reveals a much more serious problem.

For reasons that appear to be deeply rooted in our evolutionary biology, we are more confident in our judgments and knowledge than objective facts give us any right to be. This leads to results that couldn't be more serious. For a particularly sobering view of the problem see Johnson, *Overconfidence and War* (2004).

For our purposes, overconfidence leads to negotiators who overestimate their talent and their likelihood of success. Sometimes, if there is only one overconfident competitor in a negotiation, that trait can be an asset: It intimidates opponents and makes bluffs more effective. But when there are two, the risk is an expensive and time-consuming deadlock even when mutually beneficial outcomes would have been possible.

There is a difference between being overconfident and appearing overconfident, and there are two views on the question of which is better. One view, held by Shell and explained in *Bargaining for Advantage*, is that it is fine to appear totally confident when your task is to rally the troops or to intimidate the enemy. But, in private, Shell says, cool calculation of cold reality is best.

Johnson, in *Overconfidence and War*, has a different view. He says the effective kind of overconfidence, the kind that really convinces opponents you are stronger than they are and gets them to back down, is self-deceptive overconfidence. In order to tell a really convincing lie, in other words, you need to believe it yourself. Johnson believes evolution has shaped our thinking in conflict situations in just this way.

I once saw an example of this in a negotiation class. I divided the students in pairs, gave them a simple sale-and-purchase negotiation exercise, and told them to make a deal. One seller came back with a deal that was many times better than any of the others. Instead of a sales price in the thousands of dollars, his was in the tens of thousands. It turned out he had misread the instructions and set his target price an order of magnitude higher than he was supposed to. His opponent, who was reading her instructions correctly, was so intimidated by his confidence that she believed she must have misunderstood something. She allowed his inflated opening price to anchor her subsequent bargaining, and she gave away the store. "He seemed so sure," she said.

While it may have led to a desirable outcome for the seller in this exercise, I do not suggest that inability to read and understand simple instructions is a good long-term strategy. The ability to appear more confident than you are is certainly an asset. But Johnson's point and mine is that self-deception, even if it was adaptive in the Pleistocene and even if it might be helpful today in that moment just before a fight breaks out in a bar, is not an adaptive strategy in most of the contexts likely to confront readers of this book.

People in general are overconfident. My guess is that lawyers are more overconfident than others. We are paid to support our clients and our client's views of the world. Our clients depend on us. Our incomes depend on our success in representing their interests. These facts distort our view of our clients' cases. Part of correctly evaluating a case in preparation for settlement negotiations includes adjusting for that distortion.

§2.01(d) Self-Serving Bias

Think of a horse barn. Suppose there is a stall in that barn that badly needs to be mucked out. Someone has to shovel out all the nasty old straw or sawdust, cart it off in a wheelbarrow, and put down a fresh new layer. What would be a fair price to pay someone to do that?

Now, how much would someone have to pay *you* to do it?

If there is a difference between those two numbers, and I suspect there is, how do you explain it?

The difference between what you think is a fair price to pay "someone" to perform a task and what you think is a fair price for *you* to perform it is a member of a family of psychological features. Overconfidence and the Lake Wobegon effect are also members. We can call the family **self-serving bias**. As we will see, it is a large family.

The degree to which our thinking is biased in our own favor is hard to exaggerate. We judge the letters that appear in our names to be more attractive than the letters that don't (Fine, 2006, p. 4). One study asked hypertension patients, "Can people tell when their blood pressure is high?" Eighty percent gave the medically correct response: no. But asked whether they could judge their own blood pressure "What about you? Can you tell?" 88 percent said yes (Myers, 2002, p. 78).

Ninety percent of Americans believe their peers are too fat, but only 40 percent believe they themselves are too fat. This amazing statistic comes about in part because when we calculate our body mass index we add "phantom height." Women, on average, add an inch. Men add two ("Everyone's fat but me, Americans say in poll." April 13, 2006 *Sydney Morning Herald*).

"In a final irony," Cordelia Fine says in *A Mind of Its Own: How your brain distorts and deceives*, "people think that others are more susceptible to the self-serving bias than they are themselves" (2006, p. 8).

Another aspect of self-serving bias is a psychological tendency for each of us to see himself as representative of the norm. My use of "himself" in that last sentence is itself an example of what I'm talking about. I am male. I see the world from a "male perspective." We could argue for a long time about what that means, but it means at least this: that I think of being male as being the norm. When I say there is a psychological tendency for each of us to do something, the "each of us" I have in mind is male like me.

I mention this not because I'm interested in making a case for non-sexist language or political correctness. I mention it because the tendency to see ourselves as the norm is a potentially dangerous mistake in thinking.

I remember being in the locker room at the Y and talking to a guy who had what I considered to be a perfectly developed body. I've been working out for years, but I still carry around several pounds I would rather not. I would rather look like this guy, so I asked him what his workout regimen was. He said it was "nothing excessive." Swim a few miles in the morning, lift weights at lunch, bicycle for a few hours after work, run 10 or 15 miles on weekends. Nothing excessive.

We tend to believe "less than me is not enough, more than me is too much." If you change your oil or clean your bathroom or tip your waitress more than I do, you're overdoing it. If you exercise or read the paper or call your mother less than I do, you're slacking. We all have a tendency to think that way, and it leads to problems.

The guy who designed your DVD player knows a great deal about DVD players. No doubt he has been programming them and designing them and tinkering with them for years. The steps you have to go through to record a show next Wednesday at 6 PM are perfectly self evident to him. That's fine unless he makes the mistake of thinking that what is self evident to him is self evident to the rest of us. It isn't. (For a brilliant discussion of the infuriating consequences of this mistake, see Donald Norman's *The Design of Everyday Things*.)

This combination of psychological tendencies — self-serving bias, overconfidence, and ignoring of base rates — causes a phenomenon I have seen over and over again with students in my negotiation classes. Replicating a famous experiment, I pass out sheets describing the fact pattern in a hypothetical lawsuit. Then I ask my students to assess the plaintiff's chance of winning and to estimate the likely recovery. All the fact patterns are identical. I don't tell them, however, that half the sheets begin with "You represent the plaintiff in this matter" while the other half say "You represent the defendant in this matter." What result?

My rigorously trained, logical, analytical law students, who have nothing at stake and who have been conditioned to suspect a trap whenever I give them an exercise, nevertheless average a greater recovery for the plaintiff when they are told they represent the plaintiff than when they are told they represent the defendant. Invariably.

If I get such a robust effect under those conditions, imagine how large the effect is in the real world where people are playing for real money.

§2.01(e) Endowment Effect

Human beings tend to overvalue anything perceived as "mine."

> It is in the nature of a man's mind. A thing which you enjoyed and used as your own for a long time, whether property or opinion, takes root in your being and cannot be torn away without your resenting the act and trying to defend yourself, however you came by it.
>
> - O. W. Holmes (quoted in Thaler, 1992, p. 76)

This is called the **endowment effect.** An easy way to see how it works is to pick something that belongs to you and ask yourself two questions about it. Pick your house, your car, or your laptop — any non-trivial object will do. Ask yourself, What is the least amount of money I would accept to sell this thing? Then ask yourself, If I didn't already own it, what is the greatest amount of money I would pay to buy it?

Classical economics says the answer to the two questions will be the same. The value of an object to you is the price at which you would be equally willing to buy it or to sell it — the **indifference point**. It's related to the way we assure that the division of one cookie between two children is fair. If one child cuts the cookie and the other chooses first, the cutter will try to cut at the point where she is indifferent to which piece she winds up with. The indifference point is, by definition, the fair point of division. But it turns out that isn't the way people think about objects that belong to them. The way we actually think, the indifference point moves.

If you are like most people, there is a difference between the amount you would sell your laptop for and the amount you would pay to buy it. The smallest amount you would accept to sell it is greater than the largest amount you would pay to buy it. Because of the endowment effect you would not be able to make a deal with yourself!

This is not rational. A rational economic actor places a value on an object. He does not first have to ask, Is it mine?

The classic endowment effect experiment was done by Richard Thaler and colleagues at Cornell (Thaler, 1992, p. 63). Thaler did his experiment with Cornell mugs and pen sets. I have done a simplified version using sleeves of golf balls. As people come into the room, half of them are randomly given a sleeve of golf balls as a gift. I explain that there wasn't enough in the budget to give golf balls to everyone but that there will be a chance to rectify matters. I ask the people who got the golf balls to write down the smallest amount they would accept to sell them, and ask the people who didn't get them to write down the largest amount they would be willing to pay to buy them.

What would we expect to happen? Since the golf balls were distributed randomly, we would expect that some people who got golf balls don't want them and some people who didn't get golf balls do want them. We would expect there to be a market. But when I average the prices demanded by the sellers and compare it to the average price the buyers are willing to pay, I consistently find no overlap. Just as Thaler found in his experiments, my sellers tend to want roughly twice as much to sell their golf balls as buyers are willing to pay to get them.

Note that the effect is almost immediate. Only seconds after receiving their golf balls, the subjects in my experiments placed roughly twice the value on them that the people who did not receive golf balls did.

Not long ago I was giving a talk on this subject, and I realized I had neglected to bring anything to demonstrate the effect with. I was inspired to give half the audience members an imaginary school sweatshirt. The effect was the same as with golf balls. People who received an imaginary sweatshirt demanded, on average, twice the amount of money to sell it that those who did not get one were willing to pay. They had become attached to an imaginary object they had pretended to own for two minutes.

I had a chance to observe this effect in my own life. I opened the mail one day and found a check for $3,000 from my friend Lawyer B. I thought it was a mistake and called Lawyer B to ask about it. He said it was a referral fee. It seems many months earlier my wife told me about someone she knew who had been badly hurt in a biking accident. This person was looking for a lawyer to sue the bike manufacturer. I suggested my friend Lawyer A. Lawyer A, in turn, suggested our mutual friend Lawyer B. Lawyer B filed suit and got a substantial settlement with a one-third contingent fee. He sent Lawyer A and me each half of one third of his fee. (This is kosher in Michigan. We are a peer referral state.) I thanked Lawyer B enthusiastically and hung up the phone. But about 10 seconds later I wasn't so delighted. How come I had to share my money with Lawyer A? He didn't do anything.

When my wife got home I told her all about it, including how interesting it was that the endowment effect attached so quickly. Money I didn't know about and wasn't expecting one minute became *my* money the next minute, and I resented having to share it.

"Share it?" she said. "It doesn't have anything to do with you." And with that she picked up the check, put it in her pocket, and I never saw it again.

* * *

Here's an easy endowment-effect thought experiment. Consider the contents of the top drawer of your desk. If your desk is like mine, it contains several unidentified keys, scraps of paper with names and phone numbers from unknown people, business cards from forgotten meetings, a number of pieces of plastic that must have broken off of something or other, some pens that don't work, some pen parts, a cheapo key ring, assorted nuts and bolts, a piece of ancient candy, and so on. A buncha crap, to use the technical term.

Suppose there was a knock at your door and someone stood there with a box containing all that stuff and he offered to sell it to you. "Hi there, wanna buy a box of crap?" You'd probably call a cop.

But suppose your spouse decided to tidy up the place and cleaned out your drawer and threw your crap away. What result?

This little thought experiment shows the power of the endowment effect. People value things that belong to them. It doesn't matter what it is or how long they have had it. Things that are theirs are valuable.

We can do some speculative evolutionary psychology to provide an explanation for why this effect exists. In the ancestral environment it was likely an adaptive strategy to care deeply about your stuff and to resist forcefully anyone who wanted to take it from you. Given a population that cared deeply about its stuff and another population that was more blasé, the blasé folks likely did not survive long enough to reproduce and become our ancestors.

That's fine. But our evolutionary ancestors are not the ones negotiating the settlements of our lawsuits. The effective negotiator (let's call him or her "EN" for short) would be aware of that and adjust for it. The endowment effect causes people to put undue value on things that belong to them. It accounts for some of the value your opponent puts on his case, and it accounts for some of the value you put on yours.

As we shall see, the principle applies not just to physical stuff. As Mr. Justice Holmes said in the quotation above, it also applies to opinions.

§2.01(f) Illusion Of Control

Another psychological feature affecting the way we evaluate cases is called the **illusion of control**. Experimenters testing this effect asked subjects how much they would be willing to bet on horse races. In one experimental condition, the horse race had already taken place but, of course, the winner was not known. In the other condition, the race had not yet been run. People, it turns out, are willing to bet significantly more on a race that has not yet taken place than on one that has. Why? There is really only one answer. We believe that our betting on a race can have an effect on the outcome (Bazerman & Neale, 1992, p. 61).

Evidently, we do not believe that our bet can have an effect on a race run yesterday, though it is hard to understand why not. Once magical powers are accepted, it seems rather arbitrary to limit the effect to races to be run in the future. But there it is. It's a powerful idea. "We want to, and think we can, control chance events" (Kida, 2006, p. 87).

- State lotteries in North America did not become popular until New Jersey introduced a game that allowed players to choose their own numbers (Thaler, 1992).
- People will demand more money to sell a lottery ticket if they picked the numbers than if they didn't (Kida, 2006, p. 87).
- Gamblers are willing to bet more on the roll of dice they themselves throw than on dice thrown by other people or by mechanical devices (Langer, 1975).

We are all, I think, familiar with this kind of magical thinking. Let's use the dice example. We want to roll a seven very badly. We blow on the dice. We talk to them: *C'mon bones, baby needs new shoes!* We concentrate on visualizing our success as our visualization coach instructed us to do. We *will* the dice to land on seven. We rattle, we yell *Hah!* and we throw… *seven!* A winner!

The human brain is very good at seeing patterns and at finding causal relationships. That ability is a good part of why we are here having this conversation. Our ancestors saw patterns of causation that allowed them to avoid poisonous plants and venomous snakes. But we are also prone to commit the logical fallacy *Post hoc ergo propter hoc* — "After this, therefore because of this." We see patterns and draw causal inferences where patterns and causation do not exist.

We wanted the seven very badly. We could *feel* how badly we wanted it. When the seven came up, the conclusion the brain wants to draw is that there is a causal connection between the feeling and the seven. I willed the seven.

Actually, our magical ability involves more than force of will and telekinesis. Careful measurement has shown that people roll the dice harder when they want a high number and more gently when they are looking for a low one (Plous, 1993, p. 171).

§2.01(g) Belief In A Just World

In the Middle Ages, one way lawsuits were decided was by burning both litigants with a hot iron. The wounds would be bandaged, and a specially trained man would examine them after a prescribed period. The party who had healed better was believed to be favored by God and was therefore the one telling the truth.

We don't settle lawsuits that way anymore, but the idea persists. Despite centuries of evidence to the contrary, we have a deep-seated desire to see the world as an orderly and rational place and to believe that goodness (especially mine) is rewarded and evil (especially the other guy's) is punished. What goes around comes around. "No man in the wrong can stand up against a fellow that's in the right and keeps on a-comin'." We were all raised on some variant of that unofficial motto of the Texas Rangers. It isn't true, of course, but that has never been the point. It builds confidence, and confidence increases reproductive success.

I recently found myself in a conversation with a young woman who had just learned she was pregnant. It was somewhat problematic, she said, because she had been dating the baby's father for only six weeks. She didn't think she was ready to have a baby. "But," she told me, "evidently my body did." She then explained that the pregnancy was "meant to be" and concluded, "Things happen for a reason."

She is perfectly correct, of course. Things do happen for a reason. The reason pregnancy happens is, I would have thought, particularly well known.

§2.01(h) Fundamental Attribution Error

When I'm looking for reasons to explain why I did something, the reasons I come up with are different than the reasons I use to explain why you did the same thing. If we have a meeting and you are late, my explanation is that you are careless, unreliable, thoughtless, and disorganized. I was late because there was a traffic jam.

The double standard underlying this kind of thinking is called the **fundamental attribution error**. The reasons for your failures are part of *who you are*. You are a lazy, thoughtless, and untrustworthy person. The reasons for my failures are *external* to the real me. They have nothing to do with the type of person I am. I am a wonderful type of person. When I fail it is because there was a train blocking traffic, or the test was unfair. It is *not my fault*.

Interestingly, with respect to successes the situation is reversed. When you succeed, it is because of situational circumstances external to you. You happened to be in the right place at the right time. You went to school with the boss. You got lucky. When I succeed, it is because of who I am — internal resources, strength of character, that kind of thing. I am completely entitled to the credit.

> Athletes attribute their wins to themselves and their losses to bad officiating. Students who perform well think a test is a valid assessment of their ability, while those who perform poorly think the test is unfair. Teachers believe that their students' successes are due to their teaching skills, while their students' failures are due to the students' lack of ability or motivation. If the manuscript is rejected for publication, researchers think it's due to the arbitrary selection of a particularly critical reviewer, as opposed to the quality of what they wrote. (Kida, 2006, p. 158)

For many years I worked for Coleman Young, the uniquely colorful mayor of Detroit. The most disparaging (printable) thing the mayor could say about another politician was, "He couldn't get elected if his mama counted the votes." Like several of the other psychological effects we have discussed, the fundamental attribution error is another way we all let our mamas count our votes.

§2.01(i) Availability Heuristic

Ask yourself this question: What percentage of the housework do I do? Write that number down so there can be no cheating. Now go ask the people you live with to answer the same question for themselves and to write their numbers down. Add the numbers up. More than 100 percent, isn't it?

Part of this can be explained by the way the data come in. Every time I take out the garbage or empty the kitty litter, I have to stay right there for the entire grueling operation. When my wife does it, it seems (to me) to happen by itself. The box was full, and now it's empty. Easy. The floor was muddy, and now it's not. Like magic. My contributions take up more mental space than hers. I look at the area covered by memories of me working and compare it to the area covered by memories of her working, and I come up with an estimate of our relative contributions. Oddly, it is an estimate with which she disagrees. This process has a fancy name, naturally. The tendency to mistake the most available information for the most relevant information is called the **availability heuristic**.

The availability heuristic is what causes us to fear the wrong risks. Here's a test. From each of these three pairs, choose the one that is the more common cause of death in the United States:

poisoning	or	tuberculosis
homicide	or	suicide
all accidents	or	stroke

Most people choose the first term in each pair. But it is the second cause that is more common.

Remember the central idea of evolutionary psychology: We are the inheritors of minds formed when humans lived in hunter-gatherer bands. We are adapted to living in groups of 100 to 150 people. Once a group gets much larger than that, it becomes difficult for everyone to know everyone else. Since we are likely to work best, work hardest, make the most sacrifices, and take the most risks on behalf of people we know, it makes sense that groups of 100 or so are among the most efficient organizations. Military organizations, for example, have been organized into groups of 100 soldiers since the days of the Roman centurions.

In a group of 100 people, there aren't very many freak accidents. In the ancestral environment, if you hear somebody got eaten by a shark, then: (a) it will be somebody you know, and (b) it makes good sense for you to be afraid of sharks. Today if any one of six billion people gets eaten by a shark, you are likely to hear about it. Because the brain we have is the one we inherited, the brain processes that information the way our hunter-gatherer ancestors would have processed it. We are afraid of being eaten by sharks.

Let's do the math. Suppose on any given day there is a 1 in 100–million chance that someone will accidentally poke his eye out with a stick. In a group of 100 people, that translates to one occurrence in a million days or roughly 3,000 years. In a world with six billion people, a 1 in 100–million occurrence is likely to happen 60 times a day. And with television and camcorders and YouTube, it's likely that someone will post a picture of it. The ancestral brain doesn't know about YouTube. When it sees something, it reacts as though the thing it's seeing were happening in real time and real space. It thinks it makes sense for you to be afraid. As recently summed up by David Myers: "We fear what our ancestral history has prepared us to fear. ... We fear what we cannot control. ... We fear what is immediate. ... We fear threats readily available in memory." (Myers, 2007).

§2.01(j) Probability

We're altogether bad at determinations of probability. Think of the number of people who bet on the California Lottery. The odds of winning are one in 18 million. A person is nine times more likely to die by falling out of bed. It is interesting to notice that the winning lottery ticket is the one that chooses the correct 6 numbers from the integers 1 through 56. Few of us are capable of figuring out the odds of making that selection correctly. And that is precisely the point. If someone said, "I am thinking of a number from 1 to 18 million, see if you can guess what it is," not many people would bet they could guess right (Burnham & Phelan, 2000, p. 85).

In a delightful 1994 book called *Inevitable Illusions* by a scholar with the delightful name of Massimo Piatelli-Palmarini, the following law appears: "Any probabilistic intuition by anyone not specifically tutored in probability calculus has a greater than fifty percent chance of being wrong" (p. 132).

"In other words," he explains, "it is always more likely that our probabilistic intuition will be wrong than [that] it is right." See *Innumeracy* by John Allen Paulos (1990) for a thoroughly engaging discussion of this problem. The difference between our instinctive

System 1 reaction to probability problems and our rational System 2 reaction (as well as most of the other ideas discussed in this book and many that are not) is also the central theme of both *Fooled By Randomness* and *The Black Swan* by Nassim Nicholas Taleb.

§2.01(k) The Conjunction Fallacy

In a famous experiment, Daniel Kahneman described a woman named Linda: "Linda is 31 years old, single, outspoken, and very bright. She majored in philosophy. As a student, she was deeply concerned with issues of discrimination and social justice, and also participated in anti-nuclear demonstrations."

As Kahneman's subjects did, take a moment to rank the following statements about Linda in order of their probability, 1 being the most probable and 8 the least probable.

a. Linda is a teacher in an elementary school.

b. Linda works in a bookstore and takes yoga classes.

c. Linda is active in the feminist movement.

d. Linda is a psychiatric social worker.

e. Linda is a member of the League of Women Voters.

f. Linda is a bank teller.

g. Linda is an insurance salesperson.

h. Linda is a bank teller and is active in the feminist movement.

The statements we are interested in here are **c**, **f** and **h**. The rest are included just to make the question less obvious. Most people figure statement **f** is less likely than statement **c**. Linda is less likely to be a bank teller than active in the feminist movement. That's not surprising. What is surprising is that many people rank statement **h** as more likely than statement **f**. That is, they say it is more likely that Linda is a bank teller and active in the feminist movement than it is likely that she is a bank teller. A moment's reflection shows this is impossible. Linda can't be a feminist bank teller without being a bank teller.

If Linda is a feminist activist and has to work as a bank teller to pay the rent, we can tell ourselves a story about her that is consistent with our stereotypes. The story without the feminism is less compelling as a narrative because it clashes with our stereotype of a bank teller. And when logic clashes with stereotypes or other heuristics, logic loses.

People are willing to pay more to buy flight insurance that will cover them for death by terrorist attack than they will pay for coverage for death by any cause. If you ask people how many murders there are annually in Michigan, they say 100. If you ask them how many there are in Detroit, they say 200.

What's going on here? Storytelling is trumping both facts and logic. As is so often the case, System 1 is trumping System 2.

§2.01(l) Status Quo Bias

In a famous experiment by Samuelson and Zeckhauser, subjects were told they had just inherited a significant sum of money and were given a choice of four types of investments. They could choose between investing in tax-free municipal bonds at 6 percent, Treasury bills at 9 percent, a stock with moderate risk and a moderate expected return, or a stock with higher risk and a higher potential rate of return. About a third of the subjects chose to invest in the moderately risky stock, about a third chose the munis, 18 percent chose the risky stock, and 18 percent chose the T-bills.

The experimenters ran the test again, but for the new subjects a status quo was established: They were told the money was already invested in one of the four options. Subjects were then told they could leave the money where it was or move it (without cost) to any of the other options.

What result? Logically, you would think people would move the funds to the option they preferred, but that isn't what happened. What happened is, "No matter which investment option was presented as the status quo, it was the favorite choice of subjects in each group" (Belsky and Gilovich, 1999, p. 93).

There's an old joke about stock brokers. A guy calls up his broker and says, "What do you think about AT&T?" Broker says, "Do you own it?" The joke is funny, to the extent it's funny, because the broker is supposed to have an opinion about AT&T independent of whether the customer owns it, that is, independent of whether he can make a commission trading in or out of it. The fact is, neither the broker nor the customer think of it that way.

We have a bias in favor of the status quo. Perhaps it is related to our belief in a just world. Many of us feel strongly that things are the way they are for a reason and that change is bad. Partly it is laziness, partly superstition, partly habit, but we feel that it is best to leave things alone to let them work themselves out. Things are the way they are meant to be.

I feel that way about furniture. From time to time my wife will ask what I think about moving a couch or a chair from one place to another. I never think it's a good idea. I think the couch is where God wants it to be. If He wanted it to be somewhere else, it would *be* somewhere else. After it is moved, I quickly come to feel the same way about the new location and resist moving it back.

The **status quo bias** prevents us from settling lawsuits. We believe in letting nature take its course and we are reluctant to interfere.

In a lawsuit, both parties have a status quo: They are on the road to trial. And where there is a status quo, there is a status quo bias. Getting off of the road to trial and working to settle the case require the parties to abandon the status quo. As we have seen, this can be especially difficult, especially when it is bound up with belief in a just world. Many litigants believe if they can only get their day in court, the wise magistrate will make everything better. It's quite touching, really. EN attempts to manage this perception. He might remind his client, as the immortal Fred Rodell said, "A judge is just a lawyer who knew a governor" (Rodell, 1939/1980, p. 24).

§2.01(m) Regret Aversion

Imagine two brothers, Alphonse and Bocephus. Their Great Aunt Carla died and left them each 1,000 shares of Amalgamated Consolidated valued at $50,000. Alphonse left the money in Amalgamated Consolidated. The stock went down in price and he lost $25,000.

Bocephus sold his Amalgamated Consolidated and bought United Affiliated stock instead. United Affiliated also went down in price, and he also lost $25,000.

Who do you think feels worse?

Once more, the answer we get from classical economics is that both brothers should feel exactly the same. They feel like people whose investment decisions lost them $25,000. But the behavioral economics answer is different. It turns out most people think Bocephus would feel worse. This is because most people place a different value on a case where they do nothing and it turns out badly and a case where they do something and it turns out badly. It is hard to explain why this should be so, but most of us feel that way.

This is called **regret aversion**. Alphonse chooses to leave his inheritance invested where it is because he knows he will regret it more if he acts and loses than if he doesn't act and loses. He makes his choice to do nothing in order to protect his psychological downside. He "lets nature take its course" because in the end it will be nature and not he who takes the blame.

§2.01(n) How To Deal With 2.01(a)-(m)

First, let's review the psychological factors that are preventing your opponent from realistically evaluating his case.

- He thinks he is more talented than he is (the Lake Wobegon Effect).
- He thinks he is more likely to prevail than objective reality would indicate (overconfidence, partly as a result of ignoring base rates).
- He believes his case is worth more than it is simply because it is his (endowment effect).
- He believes he can control future events by force of will (illusion of control).
- He believes he will prevail because he is right (belief in a just world).

- He believes he has gone over all the relevant facts objectively and carefully, and that they support his view of the case (self-serving bias and availability heuristic).
- Even if the chances of prevailing and the range of likely recoveries have been explained to him, he can't evaluate them properly because he doesn't understand probability.
- He's a sucker for narratives to the point where they can overcome elementary logic (the conjunction fallacy).
- Finally, he is reluctant to do anything to interfere with the way the gods have ordered the universe (status quo bias and regret aversion).

Against that array of distortions, illusions, and incompetencies, it's amazing we are ever able to settle at all. But here's the hard part: It's not just your opponent's case valuation that is affected by this list of biases and cognitive errors. So is your client's valuation. And so is yours.

A case I had some years ago stands out in my mind as a model of every one of these problems. The claimant alleged he had been laid off as a result of his disability. I was mediating the case for the Equal Employment Opportunity Commission ("EEOC").

The claimant was a pleasant enough fellow, but the case was entirely without merit as far as I could tell. The employer said, with what I judged to be complete credibility, that the firm had no idea the man was disabled. There was no evidence at all to rebut that claim. Further, at the same time the employer laid off the claimant, it laid off all its other employees in the claimant's classification (and several others besides) as a result of a business downturn.

Nevertheless, the employer was willing to make a settlement offer in the case because it didn't want to have an unknown liability on its books during discussions with a potential buyer.

In other words, I could get the guy a nice settlement if he would let me. I explained about the Americans with Disabilities Act and about his likelihood of recovery. I explained about motions for summary disposition. I explained how long it takes to get a case to trial and the vagaries of the jury system. I explained about court costs and attorney fees. And I presented the offer.

He appreciated it, he said, but I was wasting my breath. He wasn't pursuing this matter for himself; he was doing it for disabled people everywhere. It didn't matter if he won or lost. What mattered was that he was doing what was right. And he had promised God that he wasn't going to settle no matter what they offered.

Elsewhere in this book I will tell stories where I was a hero. This is not one of those. I couldn't get the guy to be such a profound disappointment to God.

* * *

One way a lawyer (or a mediator) can influence a litigant to adopt a more worldly view of the prospect of settlement is through a process I call recasting.

The client is doing a great deal of self-talk reaffirming his role in his lawsuit. As it stands, he sees himself as the Avenging Sword of Justice. The goal of recasting is to change the role he talks to himself about. You want him to cast himself instead as the Reasonable Adult.

It is important to do this early. Once the role is cast, it is difficult to change. You do have a couple of things going for you, though. The client came to you because you have credibility; you are the expert. You wear the uniform, you have the badges and indicia, the dark suit, the big desk, and the thick books. He wants this meeting to go well. He wants you to like him and to agree with him. He wants you to agree with him so much that he will change what he thinks to get it to coincide with what you think. This is the **affirmation bias**, and it is very strong. So you might say something like this:

> "Well, Mr. Client, I see you have a worthwhile case and I'm looking forward to helping you get it resolved. I want you to get the best result you can, and I'm going to work hard to see that you get it.
>
> "But, as I'm sure you understand, the justice system in America is not a perfect system. We're going to get the best outcome we can get. We can't expect to get the best outcome we can imagine.

> "You know, sometimes I see people who are in love with their lawsuits. These are people who have so little going for them that their lawsuits become the main focus of their lives.
>
> "I can tell from talking to you, Mr. Client, that you are not one of those people and I want you to know I appreciate it. You are obviously a sophisticated adult with a realistic understanding of how the world works. I look forward to doing business with you."

Throughout this little speech you get the client to affirm his agreement. This isn't hard. Few people want to admit they have unrealistic expectations, that they have nothing going on in their lives other than their lawsuits, or that they think the justice system is perfect. No one wants to argue with a person who tells them they are realistic and sophisticated and have a mature understanding of the world.

What does this accomplish? It causes the client to rethink his role. To the extent he commits to the role of the Reasonable Adult, he will tend to behave consistently with that commitment. He will look with disdain on the deluded and childish fantasies of the client who sees himself as the Avenging Sword of Justice. "That," he thinks, "is not for sophisticated adults like me. Unlike some people (my opponent for example), I have a life to go back to when this lawsuit is over."

I'm exaggerating of course, but you get the idea. A client who wants to see himself as the Reasonable Adult and who wants to show he has better things to think about than this lawsuit is a client who can be persuaded to settle.

§2.02 THE SETUP

"The side that wants the deal the worst gets the worst deal." That's the iron law of leverage. Leverage in negotiation flows to the party with the least to lose from no deal, the party most satisfied with the status quo. If your opponent wants the deal more than you do, you get to dictate the terms.

But negotiation leverage is not a thing, it is a perception. If your negotiation opponent thinks you have it, you have it. Acquiring negotiation leverage is a matter of managing your opponent's perceptions.

To paraphrase John Hockenberry's remark, the best way to look like you have leverage is to have leverage. But it is important to understand that perceived leverage is just as good as the real thing.

* * *

One way to generate the perception of leverage is, of course, to lie. Instead of going through the trouble of getting a real job offer from a competing firm at an increased salary, you bluff. You walk into the boss's office and tell her you got another offer and you will leave if she can't beat it.

What you are attempting to convey with that move is that she needs you more than you need her. You are telling her that you have a BATNA better than the status quo. If she believes you and she wants to keep you, she will have to beat your BATNA. Note, however, there are three parts to this analysis. For you to come away with a raise, (a) she has to believe you, (b) she has to want to keep you, and (c) she has to be able to beat your alleged BATNA. If any element is missing, you just shot yourself in the head. This is a problem with lying.

* * *

Less dangerous than lying, but designed for the same purpose, is the manipulation of image. This is the reason for the interior design features of many law firms. The point of the dark paneling and sumptuous carpets, the immense conference table and the rest is to create the impression of wealth and power. The same is true of courtrooms. All that marble and mahogany is not an accident or a matter of taste. The fact that the judge is elevated and seated while the litigants are below him and standing is designed to create a distinct impression: You are a miserable supplicant; the institution is vast, awesome, and majestic. In other words, both the law firm and the court are designed to send the message that they are satisfied with the status quo. They have the leverage.

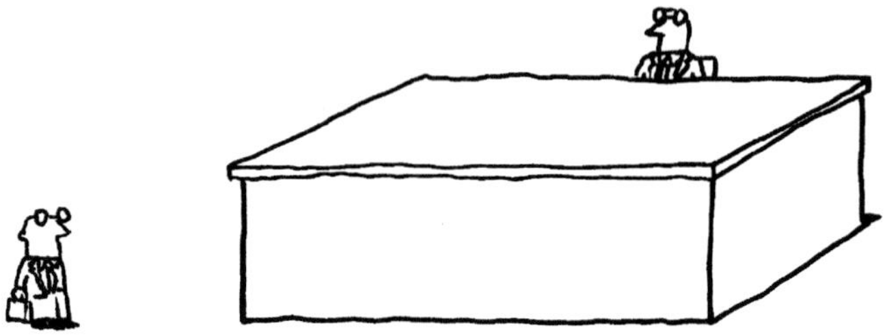

Negotiators often take a page from this book. One way to gain leverage is to look like you have it, to look like this deal doesn't mean much to you in the scheme of things. When negotiators keep you waiting in the lobby or fail to return calls or have a secretary place the call, sometimes it is because they are terribly busy with more important matters; sometimes it is an attempt to manage perceptions.

Guy walks into a new lawyer's office. Lawyer is talking on the phone and motions for the guy to have a seat. "Yeah," the lawyer says into the phone, "get me a hundred thousand shares and tell my driver to pick me up at 2:00 for that flight to London." He hangs up, turns to the visitor and says, "How can I help you?"

Guy says, "I came to connect the phone."

One impression that especially needs to be managed is that of eagerness. It is the received wisdom among many attorneys that an indication of willingness to talk about settlement is a sign of weakness. These attorneys are careful not to be the initiator of settlement discussions.

At the next level of sophistication are attorneys who approach settlement discussion with the Mature Adult posture. The message there is this: I am calling to see if you would like to discuss settling this case. This is not because I think my case is weak or because I am afraid of trial. I am perfectly happy to go to trial and I'm confident our side will prevail. I just think protracted litigation would not be the best possible use of my client's time. (Subtext: I am a practical businessperson. I know that settling meritless claims like this with bottom-feeder lawyers like you is a cost of doing business.)

There is nothing weak about that message.

What's important to recognize is that the negotiation does not begin when the parties sit down at the conference table and pull out their legal pads. The negotiation has been under way for some time by that point. If you were not aware of that, you are already losing. The negotiation began when the first contact was made. Who initiated the contact can be an indicator of where the leverage lies. If the impression is allowed to remain that the initiator is the party more eager for settlement, leverage can shift away.

* * *

If there is to be a face-to-face meeting, where will it be? Who will attend? What time? Both the answers to those questions and the path that was taken to arrive at the answers will have an effect on leverage.

Basically there are two options. You can opt for making your opponent comfortable, on the theory that you will be able to work together and problem solve for maximum mutual gain; or you can opt for making your opponent uncomfortable, on the theory that he will give you more of what you want out of fear or intimidation — or just because he wants to get the unpleasant experience of dealing with you over with. Determining in advance which option you are going to pursue will help keep your message consistent and prevent sending mixed signals.

Let's start with the uncomfortable opponent option. I'm not talking about the Tony Soprano approach to creating an uncomfortable and therefore compliant negotiation opponent. The method I have in mind is best exemplified in a classic 1947 work by Stephen Potter called *The Theory and Practice of Gamesmanship or The Art of Winning Games Without Actually Cheating.* Typical of Potter's advice are the maxims:

- "The first muscle stiffened [in his opponent by the Gamesman] is the first point gained";

- "If the opponent wears, or attempts to wear, clothes correct and suitable for the game, by as much as his clothes succeed in this function, by so much should the gamesman's clothes fail"; and
- "If you can't volley, wear velvet socks."

The idea, of course, is to put your opponent off his game, to rattle him, to take him outside his comfort zone.

Admiral Hyman Rickover, the father of the nuclear submarine, famously had several inches sawed off the front legs of the chair opposite his desk. Everyone who sat in that chair had to expend some of his mental energy keeping himself from falling forward. Other negotiators have been known to have the sun shine in their opponent's faces or have the temperature of the meeting room or the access to food or bathrooms controlled in such a way as to increase their advantage.

Meltsner and Schrag advance the same idea in a widely anthologized article called "Negotiating Tactics for Legal Services Lawyers" (reprinted in Goldberg, Sander & Rogers, 1992). Two of their suggestions are appropriate here. We will return to others later in the book. First, they suggest you arrange to negotiate on your own turf:

> Some neighborhood poverty lawyers who negotiate with attorneys for banks, realty corporations, and other large firms have added a new twist to the "home base" tactic by attempting to maneuver their adversaries into entering the ghetto, some for the first time in their lives. Their fears for their physical safety and their shock at viewing local housing conditions may reduce their bargaining effectiveness.... (p. 18).

Second, they suggest that you time the negotiations to advantage:

> When one side wants to get the discussion over with quickly, it usually loses. If you perceive that your adversary is anxious to settle quickly (or to avoid protracted discussion because his client is only paying a set fee), arrange to negotiate when you can spend a lot of time at it (e.g., when you have a whole day clear), when your adversary is pressed for time or when one of you has so

little time that, after enough discussion to whet your adversary's appetite, negotiations must be adjourned for a week or two. (p. 19)

Potter makes the same point with the maxim, "Play against your opponent's tempo." With respect to golf he advises: "Do not attempt to irritate partner by spending too long looking for your lost ball. This is unsporting. But ... the gamesman [may make] a great and irritatingly prolonged parade of spending extra time looking for his *opponent's* ball (1947, p. 35)."

People seek pleasure and avoid pain. The uncomfortable opponent is going to want to remove the source of his discomfort. He will want to get the negotiation over with and go home. As a result he will be distracted and not thinking clearly. He will make mistakes.

The other option is the comfortable opponent. There are two reasons why you might want your opponent to feel at ease. One is that he will genuinely endeavor to engage in good faith, principled problem solving in an effort to achieve maximum mutual gain. This is the advice of Roger Fisher in *Getting to Yes* and other books, all of which are wise, inspiring, and highly recommended. The other reason is that a comfortable opponent will relax his guard and make mistakes.

A third possible approach is a hybrid of the friendly, accommodating posture and the scary, threatening one. I have seen it only once, but the chill of that moment has stayed with me for 25 years. I was a very young lawyer working for the City of Detroit on a real estate development deal. My boss was only a few years older. Together we went to meet a named partner at one of the city's biggest firms. As I recall, he was tall, aristocratic, beautifully tailored, and perfectly courtly in his bearing and manner. With his great head of white hair he looked like a southern senator. He led us to a perfectly silent, dark-paneled conference room, offered us coffee from a silver service with china cups, looked us in the eye and said, "What can I do for you gentlemen?"

I don't remember anything else. All I know is that neither of us could get out of there fast enough. All we wanted was to get back to our Styrofoam cups, metal desks, familiar clutter, and noise.

* * *

There is one more finding we might touch on before we leave the subject of the comfortable or uncomfortable opponent. It is the finding that people behave much more generously when they think they are being watched. This is perhaps not surprising. We each have an interest in being perceived as generous. By operation of the reciprocity norm that we will discuss below, being perceived as generous gets us more stuff. What is surprising is that the feeling that we are being watched can be generated by a picture of a pair of eyes.

In an experiment at Harvard, 96 subjects were given a choice either to donate to a communal pot of money or to withhold their donation. Donating yielded the most money to the participants, but only if others donated as well. Half the subjects performed the experiment with a picture of a large-eyed robot named Kismet in front of them, half with no picture. The half who did the experiment with a picture of Kismet present donated 30 percent more money to the pot than the other subjects. A picture of a robot did that.

Terry Burnham, one of the scientists who conducted the experiment, believes that "even though the parts of our brains that carry out decision making know that the robot image is just that, Kismet's eyes trigger something more deep-seated. We can manipulate altruistic behavior with a pair of fake eyeballs because ancient parts of our brain fail to recognize them as fake" (quoted by Woods, 2005).

In another experiment at Newcastle University in the UK, scientists carefully clocked how much money was left for tea and coffee in the "honesty box" in the departmental coffee room. In the control condition there were pictures of flowers on the price list. In the experimental condition there were pictures of faces with the eyes looking directly out. People left 2.76 times as much money for their drinks in weeks with faces as in weeks with flowers. A 15 cm by 3 cm picture of gazing eyes tripled the amount of money people left (MacKenzie, 2006).

EN might want to keep these findings in mind when selecting the art for the room in which his negotiation opponents will caucus.

§2.02(a) Style

Another area that merits consideration in the planning phase is the question of negotiation style. Some negotiators are highly competitive, others are more cooperative. Some are inclined to joint problem solving, others more inclined to hardball tactics and intimidation. Some have high integrity, and some are less constrained. A careful negotiator attempts to learn the negotiation style of each opponent and to plan accordingly. Moreover, the careful negotiator is aware of his or her own style.

To see how awareness of style informs planning, consider a simplified universe in which all negotiators can be divided into two types, cooperative negotiators and competitive ones. That means there are four possible match-ups. When two cooperative negotiators meet, they will get a deal. When two competitive negotiators meet, they often will not. Each will puff and posture and paw the earth until he drives the other one away. When a cooperative meets a competitive, though, the advantage goes to the competitive negotiator. He will lie, and the naive cooperative will believe him. He will pound on the table, and the cooperative will give in. This sets up a situation we will discuss at some length when we get to the Prisoner's Dilemma in §3.03(b).

Neither the pure cooperative style nor the pure competitive style is likely to produce optimum results. The cooperatives settle too cheap. Their desire to get a deal and end the conflict prevents them from doing the hard work of searching for solutions that produce maximum mutual gains. The competitives overplay their hands and drive away too many deals that could have benefited them. The effective negotiator is aware of these different styles and how they interact.

* * *

Here are four ways to determine your own negotiation style. One way is to take the Thomas-Kilman Conflict Mode Instrument ("TKI"), available from CPP (formerly Consulting Psychologists Press) at www.cpp.com for $11.75. In the TKI, "Participants select responses from 30 statement pairs to discover which of five conflict handling styles is their preferred 'mode'." The test will reveal whether your primary approach to conflict — and therefore to negotiation — is to Compete, Collaborate, Accommodate, Compromise, or Avoid.

A second way to determine style is to administer the Mach Test, developed by psychologist Richard Christie. This test measures the extent to which the views of the subject align with the views expressed by Niccolo Machiavelli in *The Prince.* You can take an instantly scored online version of Christie's Mach IV abridged test version at http://www.salon.com/books/it/1999/09/13/machtest/. Test questions ask how strongly you agree or disagree with such notions as:

> "The best way to handle people is to tell them what they want to hear."
>
> "Anyone who completely trusts anyone else is asking for trouble."
>
> "Most people more easily forget the death of their parents than the loss of their property."

A third way to determine your negotiating style can be found in G. Richard Shell's excellent *Bargaining for Advantage* (1999, p. 9).

You are seated at a round conference table with nine other people. All the people in the room are strangers to you and to each other. Someone walks into the room and says, "I will give $1,000 to each of the first two people who can persuade the person seated opposite them to get up, come around the table and stand behind his chair. Go!" What would you do?

Shell says there are basically five responses.

- Some people won't play. They are not amused. These people are *avoiders*.

- Some people will jump up and run around the table immediately. They are *accommodators.*
- Some people will try to persuade the person opposite him to run around the table. People who try this and then give in and run are what Shell calls *compromisers.*
- People who debate and don't give in are *competitors.* The competitor will not put himself in the position where he runs around the table, but his opponent gets the $1,000 and gets to determine the split.
- Finally, there is the *problem solver.* She gets up, starts running and yells, "Quick, run around behind my chair. We can both make $1,000!"

Another negotiation researcher devised the following simple way to determine your negotiation style. Imagine you and a friend are playing a game. No money is at stake; you're just playing for fun. You will play the game five times. What win-loss-tie outcome would you prefer for yourself?

5 – 0 – 0

3 – 2 – 0

2 – 2 – 1

I have posed this question to many students over the years. It is easy to see that the people who prefer a 5 – 0 outcome are the competitive types, and that the cooperatives prefer 2 – 2 – 1. Those who prefer 3 – 2 – 0 are somewhere in between. They want to win but don't want to humiliate. What I find interesting is that the three types have difficulty explaining why they prefer what they do, or even in believing that other people can have other preferences. Competitives and Cooperatives both find it difficult to understand people who are not similarly motivated. As the proverb has it, the thief thinks everybody steals.

* * *

Once you know your negotiation style, the goal is to make adjustments based on the particular circumstances. Suppose, for example, you are a cooperative problem solver of high integrity. And suppose you learn that your opponent in an approaching, important negotiation is a competitive hardball negotiator with a reputation for dirty tricks. What then?

The simple answer is, don't go. Send your competitive hardball partner. When a street fighter is called for, you can't do better than to send in a real street fighter. And if the situation is reversed, your hardball partner should send you. A problem-solving cooperator is just going to be better at cooperative problem solving than an old-fashioned red-meat negotiator. The trick is to be aware of the difference and to make the adjustment.

The second best answer, when sending a replacement is not an option, is to be aware of the problem and to adjust your planning. The mistake that threatens the greatest harm in this situation is the belief that an effective actor against one kind of opponent is an effective actor against other kinds. A good negotiator is one who is sensitive to context and able to adjust his or her style.

§2.02(b) Plan Of Concessions

The careful negotiator has a plan that includes her aspiration point, her BATNA, and her reservation point (the price at which she will walk away), but more than that she also has a **plan of concessions**. She has an idea of an opening offer, which we will discuss in some detail in §3.01, and she has a rough map of the subsequent moves she expects from both parties. She has also taken care to consider the placement of prominent solutions in her map of concessions.

A **prominent solution** is one that automatically suggests itself. (We are indebted to Thomas Schelling for this concept, as for so much else. His book *The Strategy of Conflict* is the *urtext* in the field.)

Round numbers are a good example. How many of us stand at the gas pump and try to squeeze in an extra few drops to get the meter to stop at a nice round number like $20.00 or $30.00 or, more recently, $40.00? If my students are a representative sample of humanity, lots of us do that. But why? My students give various answers — it's easier to keep track of expenses or mileage, or it reduces the amount of change you have to carry — but I doubt these are the real answer. The real answer is that there is something psychologically satisfying about round numbers. The mind gravitates toward them.

This fact has an important effect on the choice of settlement point in many negotiations. The savvy negotiator is aware of the gravitational power of prominent solutions and knows where they are relative to her offers.

Let's see how this works. Suppose I offer my farfelator for sale for $110. How much do you think I will I settle for?

My guess is that you answered $100. If I offer it for $110 I'll be willing to take $100. Why? Is it because my initial offer was $10 higher than my reservation price? Is it because my initial offer was 10 percent higher than my reservation price?

Suppose I offer my farfelator for $80. Now what do you think I will settle for? If the way I set my initial offer is by adding $10 to my reservation price, I should be willing to settle for $70. If I set my initial offer by adding 10 percent to my reservation price, I should be willing to settle for about $73.

My guess is that was not your answer. If my initial asking price was $80 you probably thought there was a good chance I would take $50. Why?

Not because it is consistent with either of our other hypotheses about the relationship between initial offers and reservation points, but because $50 is a nice fat round number. You sense, correctly, that I feel the attraction of fat round numbers the same as you do. In a sense the deal *wants* to settle at $50. In many negotiations both parties will be willing to move substantially in order to get the settlement number to be round.

There is no rational reason for this. The dollars that make $116,428 look so messy compared to $100,000 will spend exactly as well as any other dollars. There is no economic reason for a negotiator to fight any harder or any less hard for messy dollars than for neat ones. But we do it all the time. We have psychological barriers and psychological goals way out of proportion to the value of the dollars involved.

Prominent numbers can be repulsive as well as attractive. I mediated a case recently where the defendant was adamant that the settlement would not be for five figures. The plaintiff was equally adamant that he would not settle for a penny less than $10,000. We were able to settle by moving the plaintiff's half of my fee to the defendant's bill. Why? The defendant was willing to spend more than $10,000 to settle the case. In fact he probably paid his lawyer several times what he wound up paying me even after picking up the plaintiff's half of my fee. But the settlement allowed him to stay beneath his psychological barrier in the amount he paid *to the plaintiff.*

* * *

Prominent numbers are often round, but not always. In a dispute I recently mediated, the parties asked me at 10:30 in the morning where I thought the case should settle. I said $38,484.16. After seven hours of wrangling, the attorneys on both sides cut their fees to get us there.

The case settled where it did because there was a compelling story that could justify $38,484.16 and no equally compelling story for any other number. It was a securities case in which the claimant's out of pocket loss was calculated at $76,968.32. The evidence showed two things: that the respondent brokerage should not have sold this product to this customer, and that the customer knew it was improper and held on to it anyway. Each party believed the other was 100 percent responsible for the loss, but neither wanted to go to arbitration. Blame had to be apportioned. There was simply no way either party would agree to an apportionment of blame other than 50/50. So the case wanted to, *had to* settle at a figure that represented half the loss. $38,484.16 was the only prominent solution.

The careful negotiator is aware that prominent numbers exist and that they can exert a strong attractive or repulsive force on a negotiation. She is aware of where those prominent solutions sit on her map of concessions.

§2.02(c) Stickiness

In most negotiations we expect to see a series of offers back and forth. (I use the term "offer" to refer to both offers and demands.) Many of these offers exist purely as creatures of the negotiation process. That is, they exist because the rhythm of the parties' concessions requires them. It may be clear, for example, that the deal wants to settle at $10,000. But it is also clear that it is too early in the process for an offer of $10,000 to feel satisfying. The parties need to work some more. So someone offers $11,250. No reason exists in the world outside this negotiation that would explain why $11,250 is the right place for this deal to settle. It is there so the other side can offer $8,750. *Then* someone can suggest that the parties split the difference at $10,000 and everyone can be happy.

At a higher level of sophistication, the negotiator avoids offering artificial numbers. The problem with numbers that exist purely as artifacts of the negotiation process is that they are easily ignored. Both parties know they have no justification in reality. So the prudent negotiator presents only numbers that do have justification in the real world. She will not present a number without a justification. That's another thing she does in the process of preparation. She maps out a series of concessions and an explanation for each one. Why? Because a number with a story is "stickier" than a number alone.

As we have seen, stories have gravity. They pull settlements toward themselves. We are storytelling animals. Stories have a central role in telling us about the world and how we fit into it. Litigation is largely about storytelling. Arbitration, mediation, and negotiation no less. Tell a compelling story, move the solution toward your side of the table.

Here's a little demonstration of the power of stories. Suppose there is a tennis player who starts drinking a fifth of whiskey a day. How likely is it that she will win a major tennis tournament eight months later?

Now how about this: Suppose there is a tennis player who starts drinking a fifth of whiskey a day. How likely is it that she will have a life-changing conversation with an older tennis player she knows and admires, and who is herself a recovering alcoholic; that she will join Alcoholics Anonymous; and that she will then quit drinking and win a major tournament eight months later?

Give yourself extra credit if you recognized this story as another example of the conjunction fallacy. It is mathematically impossible for the second account to be more likely than the first. The first account is true if she wins the tournament for any reason — even if she bribes the other players or poisons them. The second account is true only under very specific circumstances. But the second account feels more likely because it is a story, and we like stories (Hastie & Dawes, 2001, p. 129).

Actually, the story doesn't even have to be compelling. The mere presence of a story may be enough to change behavior. This was shown in a justly famous experiment by social psychologist Ellen Langer. Langer arranged to have the copy machines in her university library break down so there would be a line. Then she had experimenters approach people in the line and ask if they could cut in. When the experimenters said, "Excuse me, I have five pages. May I use the Xerox machine because I'm in a rush?" they got a compliance rate of 94 percent. When they said, "Excuse me, I have five pages. May I use the Xerox machine?" they got only 60 percent compliance. That is evidence that providing a reason for your request increases compliance. But here's the kicker. When the experimenters said, "Excuse me, I have five pages. May I use the Xerox machine because I have to make some copies?" they got a compliance rate of 93 percent (Langer, 1975, cited by Cialdini, 1993, p. 4).

Langer concluded that the mere presence of the word "because" increased compliance with the request. As psychologist Robert Cialdini says, "People simply like to have reasons for what they do" (Cialdini, p. 4).

Thus, a sophisticated negotiator will be prepared to give reasons for each of the offers she expects to make. Neither this suggestion nor any of the others in this book are magic; the word "because" and the addition of some random justification will not make a silly proposal into a sound one. But it does appear that the addition of a justification adds weight, adds stickiness, to a proposal. Therefore, EN (our Effective Negotiator) provides reasons for her positions at every step of the process and examines the justifications provided by her opponents.

§2.02(d) The Contrast Effect

Human beings have trouble making absolute determinations; one thing by itself is hard for us to discuss. What we are good at is relative determinations. If we can compare two things, we can say which is saltier or heavier, brighter or louder. This leads to a central insight into the psychology of negotiation: If I can control what you compare something to, I can influence what you think of it. This is the basis of many familiar negotiation techniques.

Take, for instance, the good-cop/bad-cop gimmick — an old chestnut to be sure but one that continues to pay off in interrogation rooms in police stations everywhere. The cops capture a suspect in a crime. First he is interviewed by the bad cop, who threatens him with years in prison, gang rape and beating, and so on. Then that cop leaves and the suspect is interviewed by the good cop. He is offered a cigarette and a cup of coffee. The good cop knows there must be an explanation for what happened and says he can help. If a confession isn't produced immediately, the bad cop, who has been listening from the next room, can barge in and start banging on the furniture again for a while until he is called away and the process repeats.

A cop, of course, is a cop. And if you are a criminal, cops are not your friends. But here the situation is set up so the suspect does not compare the good cop to his criminal friends out in the world; he compares him to the object that has been presented for the purpose of comparison — the bad cop. And compared to the bad cop, the good cop looks like a life saver.

The technique is exactly the same in negotiation. Meltsner and Schrag call it "Mutt and Jeff":

> Two lawyers for the same side feign an internal dispute concerning their position; one takes the hard line, offering almost no compromise, while the other appears to desire to make small concessions, and occasionally he prevails. Lawyers adverse to such a team frequently grasp at the marginal concessions because they seem substantial in relation to the position of the hard-liner. (Meltsner & Schrag in Goldberg, Sander & Rogers, p. 21)

Now consider two different scenarios (adapted from Belsky & Gilovich, 1999, p. 37). First, suppose you are shopping for a briefcase. You see one you like for $100 and you are on your way to the register to buy it when you run into a friend. He tells you exactly the same briefcase is for sale two blocks away for $75. Do you walk two blocks to save $25?

Second case. You are shopping for a couch. You see one you like for $1,000 and you are on your way to the register when you run into a friend. He tells you exactly the same couch is on sale two blocks away for $975. Do you walk two blocks to save $25?

Most people answer yes to the first question and no to the second. Even people who are too rich to care about $25 (or who see the question coming and want to confound the questioner) still sense that their "no" in the first case is weaker than their "no" in the second. The two-block walk to save $25 on the briefcase seems to make sense, while the two-block walk to save $25 on the couch seems like a waste of time.

This can't be right. The questions are the same: Would you walk two blocks for $25? Either you would or you wouldn't. What the $25 would be spent on has nothing to do with it.

But this is not how we think. It is not how the brain processes the problem. Instead we formulate the problem in our heads as one having to do with percentages. A $25 savings on a $100 item is a 25 percent discount — a good deal. A $25 savings on a $1,000 item is a mere 2.5 percent discount — negligible. I have had students who argue with me about this example. The idea is so rigidly fixed in their minds that they don't see the fallacy even after it has been pointed out.

In another experiment, subjects were asked how much they would be willing to pay to avoid standing in a ticket line for 45 minutes. It turns out they would be willing to pay twice as much to avoid standing in line for $45 tickets as they would to avoid standing in line for $15 tickets. (Kida, 2006, p. 267).

Again, this cannot possibly make any rational sense. You are you. Forty-five minutes is 45 minutes. Standing in line is standing in line. What you are standing in line *for* has nothing whatever to do with how much you ought to be willing to pay not to do it.

No matter. The point here, as in many other places in this book, is that people don't see it that way. We see things differently depending on what we're comparing them to. It's all about context. If you want to look tall, go stand next to a jockey. If you want to look short, go stand next to a basketball player.

One more example. People are invited to a free ice cream bar and told to take as much ice cream as they want. Half the guests are randomly given 17-oz. bowls and half are given 32-oz. bowls. What happens? The people with the large bowls take 31 percent more ice cream than the people with the smaller bowls. Why? Because a large bowl makes a scoop of ice cream look small. It works even if the subjects of the experiment are professional nutritionists, as they were in this example (Wansink, B., p. 67).

If you want a serving of ice cream to look small, put it in a big bowl. If you want it to look big, put it in a small bowl. We can use this insight not just on our unsuspecting guests; we can use it on ourselves. One of the main points of Wansink's book *Mindless Eating* is that we make our decisions to stop eating based on visual cues, not on the physical feeling of fullness. His experiments show that we feel just as satisfied, while eating less, if we simply eat from smaller plates.

One more old story. The young monk asks the abbot, "Is it all right for me to smoke while I pray?" The abbot says, "No way." Monk goes away. He sees an older monk praying and smoking and asks for an explanation. Older monk says, "You asked the wrong question. The question is, Is it all right for me to pray while I smoke?"

The principle in negotiation is the same. We can influence our opponent's reaction to our negotiation proposals by paying attention to the way those proposals are packaged. The careful negotiator in the preparation and setup phase begins to think about the contrast and the context he is going to establish.

§2.03 THE SCHMOOZE

Planning is over. It's time to meet your negotiation opponent for what the literature usually calls **rapport building** and what I'm calling **The Schmooze**.

If you haven't already created it, you are about to create your first impression. Like much of what your grandmother told you, what she said about first impressions is true. They *are* important and you *do* only get one chance to create one. The scientists who study these things, naturally, have a fancier way to say the same thing. First impressions, they say, establish a directional tendency. If our first impression is a good one, we tend to interpret future data in a way that will confirm our initial good impression, and to discount or ignore new information that is disconfirmatory. This is called confirmation bias; I'll come back to it in **§3.03(l).**

An elegant experiment by the pioneer psychologist Solomon Asch showed the importance of first impressions. Subjects were divided into two groups. One group was told about an imaginary person who was "intelligent, industrious, impulsive, critical, stubborn and envious." The other group was told about a person who was "envious, stubborn, critical, impulsive, industrious and intelligent." Both groups were then asked to say how happy they thought the imaginary person was, how sociable he was, and so forth. Subjects in the first group rated the person much more highly than subjects in the second group on the basis of nothing more than the order of the adjectives (Sutherland, 1994, p. 25).

Another experiment showing the same cognitive illusion is this one:

You have five seconds to estimate the answer to the following multiplication problem. Go.

$$1 \times 2 \times 3 \times 4 \times 5 \times 6 \times 7 \times 8 =$$

Write down your answer.

Now try this one:

$$8 \times 7 \times 6 \times 5 \times 4 \times 3 \times 2 \times 1 =$$

Different answers? Second one much larger than the first? When subjects are asked only one of these questions, the average answer to the first presentation of the problem (numbers starting small and getting larger) is 512. The average answer to the problem where the numbers start large and get smaller is 2,250. Interestingly, neither answer is close to the truth. The actual answer is 40,320 (Piatelli-Palmarini, 1994, p. 45).

The point is that we make very rapid initial judgments and then we approximate. Our approximations tend to be roughly "and so on in a similar way." But our approximations are not particularly good. We approximate before we know what "a similar way" is.

* * *

First impressions have power not just with respect to the quality we first noticed. Our sense of where our approximations should apply tends to expand. We tend, for example, to ascribe additional good qualities to people we have determined we like. This has a name too. It is called the **halo effect**. If we meet someone, decide we like her and that she is, say, cheerful, we tend also to think she is courteous, friendly, obedient, thrifty, brave, clean, and reverent.

This is one of those tendencies that seem to be wired into the brain. We make determinations about whether we like people very quickly. We ascribe additional good qualities to people we like with little or no supporting information. And it is hard for us to change our minds.

* * *

How quickly do we make these judgments? There is evidence that the question is resolved in a matter of seconds. One study recently showed that student evaluations of professors' teaching are the same after a semester of classes as they are after watching a video of that teacher *for two seconds, with the sound off.* (Gladwell, 2005, p. 13). We can look at a face and rate its beauty in 150 milliseconds (Etcoff, 1999, p. 7).

This makes evolutionary sense. If you accept the notion that our psychological wiring is the product of adaptation to our ancestral environment, it seems likely that early humans had to make rapid discriminations, notably between friend and foe. Guess wrong and you leave no descendants. As a result, the ability to make distinctions rapidly got selectively bred into the population.

§2.03(a) Liking

So, who do we like? The first answer is we like people who are beautiful. Even a newborn baby will gaze at the face of a beautiful person longer than at an unattractive one. The features that appear to define beauty for newborns are clear skin and bilateral symmetry.

From an evolutionary point of view, this too makes sense. Those qualities tend to show absence of disease. It's easy to see that being attracted to diseased people is not an adaptive trait. (For an extended discussion, see Etcoff's *Survival of the Prettiest.*)

There is nothing mysterious about this. Biologically speaking, there is nothing more important than reproductive success. That means part of our brain is always about the business of finding a desirable mate and making babies. When we see a member of our species who would make a high-value mate, our brains respond favorably. If the brain is pleasurably stimulated, the effect tends to spill over. This is why advertisers hire models to stand next to their products. I just opened the *New York Times* to page A2 to see if I could find an example of this. Sure enough, on the bottom of the page is a very simple ad consisting of three elements — a picture of a beautiful sexy blond, a picture of a watch, and a brand name. What is the message? If you buy this watch you get to date this model? If you buy this watch you get to look like this model? Neither of those messages makes any sense, and no one can possibly believe either claim. But the ad continues to run. And if it continues to run, it must be that it sells watches. Why does it sell watches? Because the ad doesn't work at the level of claims and their logical support (System 2). It works in the much older, pre-linguistic, pre-logical and unconscious parts of the brain (System 1).

The idea is to get the customer to associate the pleasurable stimulation with the product. If it works, we would expect to find lots of physically attractive people in, say, commission sales. If you have nothing to do one day, you can repeat the data collection I recently performed. I found myself sitting in a doctor's office for a few hours with nothing to do but people watch. The parade of fashion models I saw repping for drug companies was nothing short of astonishing. One after another all afternoon, and each one more beautiful than the last. This is not a coincidence. Even if you are a serious-minded physician engaged in the serious business of healing the sick, an attractive sales rep with a friendly smile can influence the drugs you prescribe.

* * *

Any trait that confers an advantage will spread. Furthermore, any trait that confers an advantage will be faked. If tall males are more successful, and they are, we can expect to see the invention of shoe lifts. If young people have more reproductive opportunities, we can expect to see the invention of face lifts. There are some genuinely tall people and genuinely young people. There are even genuinely friendly people. I am saying only that where a trait conveys an advantage we can expect to see more of it.

As an aside, there is also experimental support for the idea that we tend to believe in the sincerity of people who exhibit what is called neoteny, the retention of juvenile traits in the adult. We are wired to believe that babies and small animals are adorable. This makes sense, especially for babies. Evidently, we are also wired to believe that babies are innocent and honest. As a result, we tend to believe that people who have the characteristics of babies — large, round eyes and high foreheads — are sincere (Zaltman, 2003, p. 54).

§2.03(b) Similarity-Attraction Effect

We like people who are like us. This is called the **similarity-attraction effect**, and it accounts for a well-known sales gimmick. The salesman from the copier company comes into your office and notices the sailing pictures on the wall. It turns out that he is a big sailor himself. Sails all the time. Yessir.

Later in the day he will be a big fisherman, football fan, golfer, and bowler. He also has always had a deep fascination with antique cuckoo clocks. Why is this?

This is another question we can answer from the perspective of evolutionary psychology. In human beings, as well as other social animals, enormous importance attaches to in-group and out-group membership. Within the group we share, outside the group we compete. Fights within the group are largely symbolic. Fights between groups are merciless. (See Frans de Waal, *Our Inner Ape.*)

Again, in the ancestral environment it made sense to fear the stranger. It was an adaptive strategy. When we lived in groups of 100 people, if you met someone you didn't recognize, you had good reason to be afraid. Jared Diamond put it his way: "Should you happen to meet an unfamiliar person in the forest, of course, you should try to kill him or else to run away; our modern custom of just saying hello and starting a friendly chat would be suicidal" (quoted in Shermer, 2004, p. 36).

Let's think it through. Either the stranger is friendly or he's dangerous. Either you trust him or you don't. That sets up a two-by-two matrix with outcomes as follows. (We will discuss a similar matrix in §3.03(b) when we discuss the Prisoner's Dilemma.)

	Stranger proves to be	
	Friendly	**Dangerous**
Trust him	Good	Terrible
Fear him	Missed opportunity	Escape disaster

Figure 1. Outcome of Trusting or Fearing a Stranger

If the stranger is friendly and you trust him, something good can happen. You could learn something or trade your goods or have sex. But if the stranger is dangerous and you trust him, something very bad can happen. He can kill you, for instance. If the stranger is dangerous and you fear him, you increase the chances that you'll survive the encounter. If he's friendly and you fear him, you miss a chance to have a nice visit but no serious harm is done. What's a sensible *Homo sapien* to do? In general the strategy is to reduce the downside risk. Take the choice that offers the smallest chance of the worst outcome. If you fear all strangers, you reduce the chance of getting the worst possible payoff. Evolution favors that choice, and it's the choice our ancestors took. We are not the descendants of people who trusted people they didn't know.

The copier salesman's gimmick is designed to tap into this primal psychological instinct. He is not a threatening stranger from the tribe of copier salesmen. He is a fellow sailor or fellow football fan, one of us.

This is part of what is going on in the schmooze period before the parties sit down and start talking about the case. They are checking each other out to see if they are recognizable members of the tribe of, say, lawyers. This is what a necktie is for. It is a tribal marker. And we are exquisitely sensitive to it.

A careful negotiator is therefore a careful tie shopper.

* * *

The notion that we like people who are like us is also the foundation of a technique called **mirror and match**. The idea is that people who are in synch with each other will have similar posture, tone, vocabulary, and tempo in their conversation. If you train yourself to notice body language, you will often see that a group of friends talking will all be sitting in the same posture. The practitioner of the mirror and match method will consciously adopt the posture, tone, and delivery of her target. Proponents claim that in the hands of an expert the effect is hypnotic. The target gets more and more comfortable with the amazing closeness he feels toward the practitioner and allows himself to be led. Whether the practitioner is a therapist whose goal is to help or a salesman, the process is the same.

I make no claim for the effectiveness of this technique. I note only that it does appear to be consistent with what we know about ourselves. We know we are more likely to be influenced by people we like, and we know we like people who are like ourselves. It follows that we are likely to be influenced by people who are, or appear to be, remarkably similar to us.

* * *

In addition to liking people who are like us, we like people who like us. That is why salespeople are so friendly. It is why they use our first names so often. The principle is the same. People who like us are less likely to harm us. People who are perceived to like us are perceived to be less likely to harm us. We've seen this over and over. The true situation is complex. We don't have the time or mental energy to do a careful evaluation, so we depend on cues. Smiling friendliness is usually a cue that signals absence of danger. But anything that can be real can also be fake. Once the cue is identified it can be simulated, and the simulated cue will often work as well as the real one. It is best to take Lord Chesterfield's advice. "Distrust all those who love you extremely upon a very slight acquaintance and without any visible reason."

§2.03(c) Authority

We tend to obey authority and do what we're told. If the person we're dealing with has sufficient authority, we tend to *experience* what we're told to experience. Consider:

> [P]articipants in one experiment were told that a substance they would be asked to drink might induce vomiting. After drinking the liquid, nearly 80% of the participants actually vomited. When they received a placebo "antidote" to stop their vomiting, their condition improved almost immediately. As you may already have guessed, the antidote was the same inert substance but in a different color. (Zaltman, 2003 p. 62)

Again, there is probably a good reason for our obedience to authority in terms of our evolutionary history. The people with authority, old people for example, were likely to have greater knowledge. They knew from experience that when the ocean suddenly receded it meant a big wave was coming. When they told you to get to high ground, you went. The people who didn't go didn't survive to become our ancestors.

Sometimes, however, deference to authority can be a mistake. Flight recorders recovered after fatal crashes, for instance, provide plenty of examples of overly polite co-pilots deferring to their pilots.

Another problem, of course, is that authority can be faked. In the ancestral environment we knew who had authority because we knew everyone in the group. Today we identify people with authority by their badges and indicia. Medical authorities wear white coats. Judges wear black robes. Cops wear uniforms. Generals wear stars. The danger is that the badges and indicia work as a heuristic, and we trust them even when they are false. We follow the medical advice of actors dressed as doctors.

An old con called the Bank Examiner is based on our susceptibility to the influence of attire. A distinguished looking middle aged man in a dark suit turns up at old Mrs. Murphy's door, accompanied by a security officer. He explains that he is an examiner from her bank, shows some impressive looking ID, and explains that he is trying to catch an employee he suspects is embezzling money by manipulating the records of certain transactions. He thinks perhaps Mrs. Murphy's account is one the embezzler has been stealing from. If it wouldn't be too much trouble, he wonders if she would please withdraw some cash from the account so they can watch the suspect and perhaps catch him in the act.

She goes to the bank and withdraws the cash. The bank examiner and the security officer meet her back at her house. Everything went fine. There was no theft. Thank you very much. Sorry to trouble you. Everything is perfectly in order. You can put your money back in the bank. In fact, if you like, I can save you a trip and have Officer O'Connor put it back for you.

Dark suit, gray temples, shiny car, nice manners, and a friend with a uniform — that's all it takes.

§2.03(d) Food

In the ancestral environment, he who gives me food is my friend. Families get together and share food. Ceremonial occasions are celebrated with food. Few things are more culturally significant. It is not surprising that food plays an important role in the process of persuasion.

Many social psychology experiments have demonstrated this point. In one, "people snacking on peanuts and soft drinks expressed more agreement with controversial issues than those who were not given such refreshments" (Shestowsky, 2006).

Food is good — there are few statements as true as that for our evolutionary selves. As a consequence, things associated with food are also perceived as good. Things that happen to me while I am eating, including propositions that are introduced to me while I am eating, are perceived as better than those same things or propositions introduced when I am not eating. There is a reason why rug salesmen serve tea and copier salesmen take customers to lunch.

Actually, when you give me food, it sends two messages: that you are a friend, and that I owe you one. And it says both those things at a fundamental level, where I may not be aware of them. The coffee and pastries you serve at your office while we talk about the traffic or the weather or the basketball game do not take place before our negotiation. They are part of it.

During this period the effective negotiator is asking questions to find out who she is negotiating with. Are you married? Do you have kids? How old? Where do they go to school? Have you been on any interesting vacations lately? This conversation also serves two purposes. It sends the cue that the inquirer is a friend — anyone interested in my kids is obviously my friend — and it is a form of information gathering.

If I learn that you are sending three kids to college or buying a vacation house or retiring in six months, I know something that can help me later when I am formulating my offer. This is a book about the psychology of negotiation, not about tactics and strategy, so I will not concentrate on the information-gathering aspect of this conversation. But my goal as a negotiator is to produce an offer that is most appealing to you at the lowest cost to my side, and the way for me to determine what you find attractive is to learn as much as possible about who you are and what you need. You will tell me these things only if (a) I ask, and (b) you perceive me as a friend. This is why we schmooze. The effective negotiator is a good schmoozer.

* * *

There is a danger here, however. We are in the room with our negotiation opponent because there is a potential for a deal that will benefit us. We are eating pastries and drinking coffee and chatting amiably. She is a friendly sort, wearing the status markers that show she is a member of the tribe to which we belong (or aspire to belong). She is interested in us, in our career and our kids, and she shares our fascination with ice climbing or parasailing or whatever.

The danger is that she will ask for our agreement with a general proposition. The proposition will seem innocuous enough, and we will not wish to introduce a socially awkward disagreement into such a benign and pleasant conversation. This tendency to agree in order to be agreeable is called affirmation bias. A skillful opponent can use it to lead us to agree to statements we will later have cause to regret.

This is the genesis of another old salesman's trick. The salesman asks you to agree that if he can find you the car you want at the price you want, you are ready to buy today. You see no harm in agreeing. He may put it this way. He may say, "I'm looking forward to doing business with you, Mike. I can see you are the kind of man who knows what he wants and makes up his mind. You're not one of those poor hen-pecked husbands who has to check with his wife before making a decision. And you're not one of those guys who likes to spend his time shopping and dithering and never makes up his mind. You've got other things to do with your time. Am I right, Mike?"

Assuming your name is Mike, it's hard to disagree with this guy. Are you going to admit that you *are* one of those guys who has to check with his wife about every little thing? Or that you *are* there to waste his time asking questions and window shopping? Careful. Even if you see the guy as a crude sexist and a buffoon, agreeing with his statement out loud can have an effect on your subsequent decision making. It is important to understand that there is a psychological tendency to behave in a manner consistent with our earlier statements. It will be easier for the car salesman to get us to buy today if we have made such a statement than if we have not. He knows this. That's why he asked. He is looking for a commitment that he will later be able to use against you. (Give yourself extra credit if you recognized that this technique is what I was doing in Section §2.01(n) above when I talked about recasting.)

Be aware of this technique. If you agree to the statement, do it consciously and strategically. We will discuss this more in Section §3.03(k).

§2.03(e) Listening

Negotiation involves a certain amount of dissimulation. A perfectly transparent negotiator would not be a successful one. Unless you are a sociopath, however, lying is stressful. The brain has to work harder to lie than it does to tell the truth. Lying increases what the literature calls our **cognitive load**.

An increase in cognitive load is often accompanied by physical changes. That is why polygraphs work. The stress of lying causes elevated heart rate and increased sweating. It also causes what the world's leading authority on lying, Paul Ekman, calls micro expressions and micro gestures (Ekman, 1992). These are tiny movements that last only a fraction of a second. Ekman has spent 30 years studying them in slow motion. His work on the subject is fascinating. But most of us do not have the luxury of having our negotiation opponents hooked up to polygraph machines, the ability to watch slow motion video of our opponent's micro expressions, or the benefit of Dr. Ekman's training in reading them. We are going to have to rely on far less subtle **leaks**.

Some leaks are verbal. For instance, there is a difference between "I can't offer you any more" and "I can't offer you any more at this time." Or "I don't think I can offer you any more." EN pays a lot of attention to these nuances.

Other leaks are non-verbal. That's why the careful negotiator watches for changes in gesture and posture. One of the primary activities taking place during the Schmooze is that the careful negotiator is establishing a baseline. How quickly does my negotiation opponent speak? How informally? Does he have any verbal tics or pet phrases? What are his eye-contact patterns? How loudly does he speak? What do I notice about his use of gesture?

Later in the negotiation he will watch for changes from that baseline. It's not complicated. If someone says "To tell you the truth" before every sentence, it doesn't mean anything. If he never says it until a critical moment late in the negotiation, it's a stammer. The likely reason for the stammer is an increase in cognitive load. EN is alerted to the probability that the next thing out of the opponent's mouth is a lie.

The situation is similar with regard to body language. It is not true that a hand in front of the mouth means your opponent is lying or that crossing the legs means he is defensive, as the early work on body language would have it. The process just isn't that simple. But if your opponent has been leaning back and staring at the ceiling all day and now he is leaning forward and looking you in the eye, it's a good bet something has changed in the way he views the deal.

Jeffrey Krivis, a prominent California mediator, has reviewed the literature on "Interpersonal Deception Theory" and compiled this list of non-verbal leaks that may help reveal when a speaker is lying. Having established a baseline, watch for:

a *reduction* in:

- Hand gesturing

or an *increase* in any of the following:

- Pupil dilation
- Blinking
- Eye shifting (vs. eye contact)
- Fondling or manipulating (objects or parts of the speaker's own body)
- Speaking pitch
- Speech errors or "nonfluencies" (um, ah, er)
- Speech pauses
- Negatively worded statements (no, not, can't, won't)
- Foot-leg motion or rocking

(Krivis & Zadeh, 2006)

As Yogi Berra reminded us, "You can observe a lot by watching."

§2.03(f) Being Observed To Be Listening

It is not enough to listen. The careful negotiator makes sure he is observed to be listening. He shows interest. He leans forward, makes eye contact, nods, and makes affirmative-sounding listening noises. "Oh, I see. Um hum." He solicits information. "Tell me more about that." He asks open-ended questions. "Are there any other factors involved?" He paraphrases back what he has heard. He checks frequently to make sure he is receiving what the speaker is sending and to convey the message that he cares about what he is hearing and wants to make sure he's getting everything. "Let me see if I've got this right. You're an old lady. You live in a shoe. You have so many children you don't know what to do. Is that right? Hmm, I see. Can you tell me more about that? Is there something else?"

In many ordinary conversations, we listen only enough to tell when it's our turn to talk. I once took a drawing class. The professor told us that most people most of the time only look at the world carefully enough not to bump into things. He wanted us to look more carefully. I am suggesting we should listen more carefully. Make listening noises, paraphrase, and ask open-ended questions.

People like it when you listen to them. As Lord Chesterfield said, "Many a man would rather you heard his story than grant his request." Listening carefully is a kind of flattery. It will get you anywhere.

The other piece of active listening is sometimes called "validating." When EN identifies an emotion, he checks in with the speaker. "If I understand you, Mrs. Hubbard, it made you sad when you discovered your cupboard was bare. Is that right?"

This shows that the listener understands not only the facts, but the affect, the emotional component that goes with the facts. People love it when you do that. The best motto for a mediator I ever heard was "When I listen, people talk." That's the kind of listening skill we should try to develop.

3

Bargaining

We are done with preparation. We have evaluated, set up and schmoozed, and we have finally reached the point that most people would recognize as negotiating. One side is about to make an offer and the other side is about to respond.

§3.01 THE FIRST OFFER

Who is going to make the first offer, and what is it going to be? Be fore we answer those questions, it would be useful to introduce a few of the psychological principles at work in this phase of the negotiation. The first is anchoring.

§3.01(a) Anchoring

In a mock jury experiment conducted by Reid Hastie and colleagues, plaintiffs suggested either an award "in the range between $15 million and $50 million" in one condition or "in the range from $50 million to $150 million" in the other. Everything else was the same in both experimental conditions, and in both conditions the judge told the jurors, "The attorney's recommendations are *not* evidence." What result? Jurors presented with the low range returned a median award of $15 million. Those presented with the high range came in at $50 million (Hastie and Dawes, 2001, p. 106). This example illustrates **anchoring**.

We have encountered anchoring before, though we didn't use the term. When you declined to walk two blocks to save $25 on the price of a couch, it is because you were anchored on the price of the couch instead of the $25. When I said you should concentrate on your aspiration point and not on your reservation point or BATNA, I was trying to dissuade you from anchoring on the lower number. If you fall for the good cop/bad cop gimmick, you are anchoring on the bad cop. Anchors are everywhere. They're one of the design features of our judgment system.

From this, for the sufficiently devious mind, it is only a small step to the realization that I don't have to wait to see what your mind happens to seize upon as an anchor. I can plant something. Observe:

> **Question 1:** What is your estimate of the weight of the building you are now in? A rough estimate will do. Say, to the nearest 100 metric tons.
>
> **Question 2:** What is your estimate of the weight of the building you are now in? A rough estimate will do. Say, to the nearest 10,000 metric tons.

Of course I don't know what the answer is, and I don't know what your guesses were, but I am confident that the answer if I asked you only Question 1 would be significantly less than your answer if I asked you only question 2.

Why? Because you don't have a mental program for generating building weights. When you were asked to produce one you looked around the mental landscape and picked the nearest likely candidate, the anchor, and you adjusted from there. When I provided an anchor of 100 metric tons, you adjusted from there. When I provided an anchor of 10,000 metric tons, you adjusted from there.

It gets scarier. The classic anchoring experiment goes like this. Subjects were asked to spin a big wheel with numbers on it. Unknown to the subjects, the apparently random wheel was rigged to land on either 10 or 65. Then, as part of a completely unrelated task, the subjects were asked a completely unrelated question: "What percentage of the countries in the UN are in Africa?"

On average, the people whose wheel spin landed on the low number estimated that 25 percent of UN countries are in Africa. The people who landed on the higher number estimated 45 percent (Kida, p. 180).

Two distinct facts about anchoring are important. The first is that in estimating we tend to start from a reference point, an anchor, and then adjust. The second is that we fail to adjust sufficiently. Juries, for example, hand down harsher verdicts if they consider more serious charges first than if they consider less serious charges first (Kida, p. 182).

Further, we tend to adjust insufficiently from our anchors even when the anchor is conceptually unrelated to the question under consideration.

So, getting back to our negotiation, we should be acutely aware that the first number that gets put out on the table can serve as an anchor for the whole deal. It can establish the negotiating neighborhood.

* * *

I remember once asking the price of a small jade figure in an Asian art gallery in San Francisco. As I recall, the price the friendly owner quoted was two orders of magnitude greater than I was expecting. I was thinking in the hundreds of dollars; she was thinking in the tens of thousands. Since it was obvious that no amount of skillful negotiation on my part was going to get her to a sales price in my range, I smiled politely and walked out. Neither of us wasted any more time than necessary in reaching the conclusion that no deal was possible. Had I been a vastly wealthier customer, however, the gallery owner's $30,000 opening offer could have been the starting point in a negotiation. I might then have felt satisfied to get her to a deal at, say, $23,000.

The point is, if you are the party with greater market knowledge — that is, if your negotiation opponent is looking to you to establish the general negotiation neighborhood — you *may* wish to open and have your opening number serve as an anchor.

In most cases, however, you may wish to have your opponent open. Why? Because it may be to your advantage to have your opponent establish the negotiation neighborhood. Suppose, for example, that you are the gallery owner and I am selling that little jade figure instead of buying it. Suppose I'm willing to take $500 for it, and I open. I'll ask for perhaps $1,000 to make sure I leave myself plenty of room to bargain, and the deal will settle somewhere between $500 and $1,000. But if you more knowledgeably value the piece at $25,000 and *you* open, it could cost you twenty or thirty times as much.

§3.01(b) The Winner's Curse

The idea behind letting your opponent open is that you may be pleasantly surprised. If you open, the opposite may happen. Let's take the little jade again. Suppose I had picked it up and said, "This is a pretty little jade. Will you take $300 for it?" and the gallery owner had said, "Sure, cash or credit?" Suddenly my pretty little jade is not so pretty. I have the sinking feeling I overpaid.

Why? Thirty seconds ago I made an offer of $300 because I thought it was at the low end of the reasonable range. I would have been willing to pay $500, but I wanted to get it cheaper if I could. I expected my opponent to counter at, say $800 or $1,000. Instead, my opponent said "Sure" and accepted my $300. I got what I wanted for less than I expected to pay. So how come I'm not happy?

I'm not happy because of something called the **winner's curse**. When I get what I want for less than I expected to pay — when the negotiation takes fewer steps than I expected — I immediately get concerned. Either my opponent knows more than I do, and I just bought a fake or a lemon; or my opponent knows less than I do, and I could have gotten it more cheaply. In either case, I feel like a chump.

James J. White, longtime professor at University of Michigan Law School and co-author of the first negotiation textbook for law students, liked to say, "If you want to ruin someone's day, accept his first offer."

In other words, a second reason to let your opponent open first is so that, if there is going to be a winner's curse in this negotiation, it will be your opponent who suffers it, not you.

At the next level of sophistication, the really good negotiator doesn't let his opponent get the winner's curse. He adjusts his target range to allow his opponent to fully participate in the process and achieve a satisfactory result. Let's go back to my little jade one more time, again with me as the seller. I am willing to sell it for $500, but instead of opening at $1,000 I ask my opponent to make an offer. She says $25,000. If I yell "Sold" and grin like an idiot, she gets the winner's curse. Since I am a nice guy and I don't want my negotiation opponents to be unhappy, I feel it is my job is to conform more closely to her expectations. I do not want her to feel cheated; I want her to feel she got a good deal. I want her to feel she participated skillfully in structuring this deal. I want her to take ownership of the both the process and the outcome, and I want her to feel a deep sense of satisfaction. I therefore do not say, "Sold!" I say, "Make it $40,000" and then, because I remember the lesson about providing a justification for every number I propose, I point out some feature of the piece that adds to its value.

If your opponent expects a few rounds of reciprocal concessions, provide a few rounds of reciprocal concessions. My imaginary customer will feel better paying $32,000 for the jade after the negotiation she expects than she would feel paying $25,000 if I surprise her by jumping on her first offer. And I will feel better too.

I understand (because I heard it in a lecture by Nina Mierding, an expert on inter-cultural negotiation) that the same rule applies in other cultures with respect to the number of reciprocal concessions. So, for example, to a bargainer from a culture where the norm is 10 or 12 rounds of reciprocal concessions before a deal is struck, a negotiation that reaches agreement after only the two or three rounds typical of an American negotiation feels wrong. Even if the price agreed upon is acceptable, the failure to go through the customary dance makes the transaction unsatisfying.

This is another example of the good advice you got from your grandmother. That which is easily gained is lightly valued. An inheritance may be gotten hastily at the beginning; but the end thereof shall not be blessed (*Proverbs* 20:21). Since we want the results of our negotiations to be highly valued and the ends thereof to be blessed, we should endeavor to meet our opponent's expectations with regard to the number of reciprocal concessions even if we are compelled thereby to accept more or pay less than we expected.

§3.02 RESPONSES TO THE FIRST OFFER

Once the first offer is on the table, there are four possible responses. You can accept it — resulting in your opponent getting the winner's curse. You can counter-offer, which we will discuss shortly. You can walk away, as I did in the art gallery in San Francisco. An efficient negotiator, after all, is one who wastes no time on the pointless. Or, you can do none of the above. You can merely decline to respond or you can say no.

The aim of responding with silence or with no, while not breaking off the negotiation, is to move your opponent to make a better offer without an intervening offer from you. You are looking for what the literature calls a **consecutive unreciprocated concession**. In plain English, a party who makes a consecutive unreciprocated concession is "bargaining against himself." In general, as long as you can get your opponent to bargain against himself, you should encourage him to do it.

On the other hand, *you* should almost never make consecutive unreciprocated concessions. The Effective Negotiator doesn't give 'em nothin' for nothin'. This is so partly because EN is aware of the importance of his opponent's participation in the process and the resultant increased ownership of the outcome. It is also because giving away things without getting anything in return causes one to have fewer things.

That said, EN may want to consider making consecutive unreciprocated concessions under two sets of circumstances. One is when it is a strategic move designed to secure a greater concession from the opponent in another phase of the negotiation. In that case EN is not really making consecutive unreciprocated concessions at all. He is merely attempting to bank his reciprocations for a later time.

The other time consecutive unreciprocated concessions may be appropriate is in a negotiation where EN places a high value on the *relationship* between the parties and a low value on the *stakes*. Based on these distinctions, Shell (1999) provides a useful taxonomy of negotiations with appropriate tactics for each.

If I am bargaining with my wife, for example, or my 80-year-old mother, I may consider a strategy of concessions that includes consecutive concessions. The point in those negotiations is not to squeeze every possible dime out of the transaction. I love them both very dearly and their happiness is my happiness. Whatever I can do to improve their outcomes I am eager to do.

Note that it is possible to make consecutive unreciprocated concessions for one of these motives and to cause it to appear that you are making them for the other. For example, I was once involved in a negotiation for certain online dispute resolution ("ODR") training. ODR is rumored in some circles to be the wave of the future. The seller of the training sent me an email offering to refund my money if the training didn't pay for itself in six months. Before I had a chance to respond, he sent me another email offering to "make it three months." There were two subtexts to that message. One was that he was supremely confident in the quality of his product. The other was that he loved me dearly: My happiness was his happiness, and whatever he could do to improve my outcome he was eager to do.

For the record, I should confess that it worked. I paid him and took the training. Both the three-month period and the six-month period have long since elapsed. I have realized exactly zero return on my investment. The seller has been informed. He made all the appropriate noises, but as of this writing he has not yet sent the check.

What happened? He made a disarming move, a consecutive unreciprocated concession, and I was disarmed. Maybe it was sincere; maybe it wasn't. The effect is the same.

§3.02(a) The ZOPA

In a simple negotiation between a buyer and a seller, the **zone of possible agreement ("ZOPA")** is the range between the greatest amount the buyer is willing to pay (the buyer's reservation point) and the smallest amount the seller is willing to accept (the seller's reservation point). If the buyer's reservation point is lower than the seller's, there is no ZOPA and the deal will not settle. If the buyer's reservation point is equal to or higher than the seller's, then there is a ZOPA and it is possible for a deal to be reached — but it is not automatic. Bargainers typically do not reveal their reservation points. Buyers make low offers; sellers make high demands. This is perfectly reasonable, of course, but if the numbers are too exaggerated, the parties may figure there is no ZOPA and walk away.

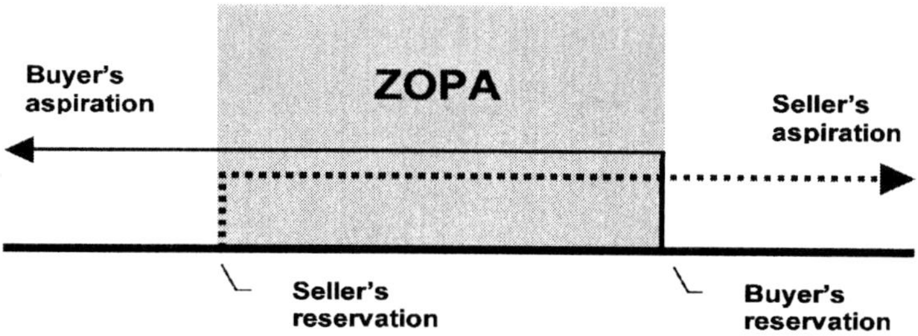

Figure 2. Zone of Possible Agreement

That's the central tension in negotiation. If there is a ZOPA, it is in the interest of both parties to find it. Concluding a deal anywhere inside the ZOPA makes both parties better off than they would be with no deal. But deals are not all the same. Sometimes the ZOPA is large, so it matters where in the ZOPA we settle. I want to settle at the end of the ZOPA most favorable to me, and you want to end up at the other end.

I want to walk away sooner rather than later if there is no ZOPA. But I want to find the ZOPA if there is one, which is going to require something like cooperation. At the same time, I want to push the deal toward my preferred end of the ZOPA, which is going to require competition. If I'm too tough, I risk failing to find the ZOPA. But if I'm too cooperative, I risk selling too cheap or paying too dear. It's tricky.

Ultimately, negotiations tend to settle at the midpoint between the buyer's first offer and the seller's first demand, if that midpoint occurs inside the ZOPA (Raiffa, 1982, p. 48). The midpoint is one of those prominent solutions we discussed in §2.02(b). We may posture for a while before reaching it, but the deal will gravitate toward that point.

This has two consequences. It means that the careful negotiator chooses his response to his opponent's first offer with an eye toward where the midpoint between those two numbers will fall. And, getting back to consecutive unreciprocated concessions, it means you will also have improved the location of that midpoint if you can get your opponent to improve his first offer before you present yours.

This is especially important if your opponent's first offer is unreasonable. As we have seen, the first number on the table has an anchoring effect. If your opponent presents a wildly exaggerated first offer, it is important that your reply be quick and clear. It can be either a correspondingly exaggerated offer, so that the midpoint between the offers falls in the ZOPA, or it can be a refusal to bargain until the opponent makes another move. What you don't want to do is leave that number out there gathering psychological strength.

§3.02(b) Alternative First Response: A Cheap Trick

A good negotiator is well advised to be aware of a cheap but surprisingly effective gimmick called the flinch. After establishing rapport, Negotiator A gets Negotiator B to make the first offer. B puts a number on the table. There it is.

No matter what the number is, Negotiator A winces.

If A has successfully established what a likeable person he is and that he is a member of the in-group rather than the out-group, B will feel the same as if he just inadvertently stepped on A's toe. In some cases B will immediately make a conciliatory concession. In others, he may need to be encouraged.

There are two basic approaches to providing that encouragement. The simpler one is to remain silent. People are uncomfortable with silence. A polite, well brought up opponent will endure silence for only a few seconds and then he will say something. Sometimes it will be a concession, other times it will be information about his position. Both, from the point of view of the flincher, are good.

The second approach is to follow the flinch with a statement. Negotiator A, looking wounded, quietly says, "Oh, I didn't realize..." and fades off.

This gambit appears most natural when used by a negotiator who holds a traditionally low-power, low-status position — a young, physically small female, for example. But it can be particularly effective if it is used by a large, high status male.

§3.03 BARGAINING CONFOUNDS

Confounding variables, known to graduate students as "confounds," are factors that sneak into experiments and screw up the results. I am calling this section Bargaining Confounds because it explores psychological factors that can enter into our negotiations and screw up our results. The first confound is the reciprocity norm.

§3.03(a) Reciprocity

In most negotiations, once there are two opening offers on the table the negotiation proceeds by means of reciprocal concessions. The subject takes us back to evolutionary psychology. Imagine again our two populations from the environment of evolutionary adaptation. Hunting is successful only intermittently, and refrigeration won't be invented for another few hundred thousand years. One population, we might imagine, is made up of individualists who eat what they kill, without sharing, and one is made up of cooperative sharers. It's easy to see that the sharers are more likely to survive food shortages and become our ancestors. This intuition turns out to be correct when the behavior of our closest relatives is studied. Not only do apes share food, but they share it preferentially with other individuals who have previously shared with them. They reciprocate. Further, apes have been shown to retaliate against individuals who do not engage in reciprocal sharing (de Waal, 2005).

But in order for sharing to develop, our ancestors had to figure out a way to solve what theorists call the first mover problem. Suppose I give you something or do something for you — I make the first move — and you simply accept what I give you and go away. If that is the anticipated response, I never do anything for you or for anybody else and we all die. That's no good.

We needed a way to ensure that the first mover will be compensated. The reciprocity norm is that solution. If I do something for you, you do something for me. This fact is built into who we are at the biological level, and it is enforced by every culture around the world. If someone gives you something, you give them something back. If you fail to reciprocate, you can expect to be punished.

This can be easily shown by experiment. Go to any bar anywhere in the world and get in a conversation. When someone at the table buys a round of drinks, accept. When someone else buys a round, accept that too. Then when everyone has bought a round but you, announce that you have something else to do and leave. See how well you are received the next time you come back.

The price of the beer is not the question here. The point is that it was *your turn* and you didn't stand your round. My guess is there is an unflattering term for such a person in every human language.

Not only will your companions resent your behavior but, more important for purposes of this discussion, you will feel uncomfortable about it too. Unless you are a lonely sociopath, you will not be proud of yourself for having put one over on the suckers at the bar. You will be ashamed — again far out of proportion to the cost of the beer — and you will seek out an opportunity to make it right. Baked into the ancient depths of your brain is the knowledge that without the reciprocity norm, we die.

As we have seen, whenever there is a strong natural response like this, someone is going to develop a way to exploit it. It's a jungle out there.

We can see this in the classic reciprocity norm experiment. The experimental subject is presented with some task or other that will take several hours. Say, rating the attractiveness of a pile of pictures. It doesn't matter. What matters is that seated next to him, doing the same task, is another person who appears to be an experimental subject but is really a confederate of the experimenters. After some time the confederate goes out and comes back with two Cokes. He says something like "I was getting a Coke so I got one for you too." More hours go by. Then during a break the confederate mentions that he is selling raffle tickets for charity and offers to sell some to the subject.

Subjects who got the Coke bought twice as many raffle tickets on average as subjects who did not get the Coke (Cialdini, p. 20).

There are two important features to notice about this experiment. One is that Cokes have nothing to do with raffle tickets. The other is that the Coke was not requested. In other words, the reciprocity norm is so strong that it is possible to get people to give you things you want by giving them things they don't want and didn't ask for.

That is why your mailbox is crowded with address labels with little pictures of bunnies on them. Whoever it is that sends those things has determined that giving away address labels generates more donations. Even though we didn't ask for the labels, and even though we have far more address labels with bunnies on them than we could ever possibly use, the arrival of yet another batch triggers the feeling that it is *our turn* and we owe the company a response. Thoughtfully, the company has provided a convenient envelope into which we can place our reciprocal gift. We don't all feel horribly guilty if we don't reciprocate. Many of us manage to cope with such guilt as we do experience. But enough of us feel enough of the pull of the reciprocity norm so that the labels pay for themselves. If they didn't, they wouldn't exist.

The reciprocity norm manifests itself in negotiation in the form of the prohibition against consecutive unreciprocated concessions. I will not bargain against myself. Once I have made a concession, it's your turn. I will not move again until you do. Correspondingly, I do not expect you to make unreciprocated concessions. If you have made a concession, you are entitled to expect me to make the next one.

The reciprocity norm can thus explain a great deal of negotiation behavior. It explains, for example, the widespread practice among union negotiators of bringing a laundry list of demands to collective bargaining negotiations. Many of these demands will have been presented to the Union by individual members and enjoy only minimal support. But they are not there on their merits. They are there so they can be conceded, and so that the concession can prompt a reciprocal concession from the employer on an issue that actually matters to the union.

It is psychologically powerful for a negotiator to say, "On point number one, we give up.... On point number two, we give up. On point number three... you should give up" (Shell, 1999, p. 231). It takes us back to the fundamental ideas of fairness we discussed in Chapter 1 and triggers the deeply seated urge to reciprocate. It's your turn. You feel the pressure of a million years of evolution telling you so.

§3.03(b) The Prisoner's Dilemma

We can deepen our understanding of the reciprocity norm if we look at the situation in a more formal way. The best way to do that is by using a device called the **Prisoner's Dilemma**. Along with the ultimatum game we talked about in §1.01, the prisoner's dilemma is probably the most common tool used to study bargaining behavior.

Imagine that the cholesterol police have been effective in their nagging and lobbying and incessant meddling in other people's lives, and now cheeseburgers are illegal. Suppose you want some anyway, and you have discovered a source. You've never met the guy before and you will probably never see him again, but he has cheeseburgers for sale and he makes you the following offer. At midnight tonight, he will leave a bag of cheeseburgers under the old oak tree on the east side of the park if you leave a bag of money under the old elm tree on the west side. What should you do?

You are a reasonable and self-interested person. You reason in a logical self-interested way. Should I trust this guy? He could double-cross me and leave an empty bag. Of course, I could double-cross him and leave an empty bag. Let's think it through. There are four possible outcomes, a two-by-two matrix. The worst possible outcome from your point of view would be if you left the money and he left an empty bag. You would have no money and no cheeseburgers. You would be a sucker. The best possible outcome would be the opposite. He leaves the cheeseburgers and you leave an empty bag. You get the burgers and you get to keep your money. He's the sucker.

If both of you leave empty bags, nobody gets hurt — there is no sucker — but nobody gets the benefit of the deal. You are in this deal because there is an opportunity for benefit, not just so you will not get hurt. You would rather have the burgers than the money and he would rather have the money than the burgers.

The final possibility is that you will each do what you agreed to do. He leaves the burgers, you leave the money.

We have entered into the realm of **game theory**, so it's time to give these things their proper names. Your options are to **cooperate** (keep your word, do what you agreed to do) or **defect** (leave an empty bag, double-cross your opponent). The worst possible outcome goes to the cooperator when his opponent defects. This is called the **sucker's payoff** and it goes, logically enough, to the sucker. The best possible score goes to the defector when his opponent cooperates. And the payoff for both players is better if both players cooperate than if both players defect. In our example, both parties would be better off if you left the money and he left the burgers than if you both left empty bags.

So, what does the rational self-interested actor do? I know my opponent will either cooperate or defect. He has to do one or the other. Suppose he cooperates, he leaves the burgers. If I know he's going to cooperate, I can either cooperate too and get the benefit of my bargain or I can defect and get the best possible outcome. Given a choice between a good outcome and a great one, I choose great. I would defect.

Suppose my opponent defects. If I cooperate, I get the worst possible outcome, the sucker's payoff. If I defect, I lose nothing. So I would defect.

If my opponent cooperates, I defect. If my opponent defects, I defect. Defecting is my self-interested, rational choice under all the possible conditions. So I defect.

My opponent, who is looking at a payoff matrix identical to mine and is just as rational and self-interested as me, defects too. What happens? We have no deal. Nobody gets suckered, but nobody benefits either.

You run into the guy again. You agree that it was too bad the deal didn't work out. You still want the cheeseburgers. He still has them for sale. You would still both benefit from a deal, and you agree to try again. You shake on it.

Now what? Look at it from his point of view. Suppose he really believes you. Suppose he is confident you will leave the money, no one will know about it, and he will never see you again. He's got the possibility of getting something for nothing. What will he do? On the other hand, you did defect on him once. He knows you are not completely trustworthy. He knows there is a chance you will defect again. If he cooperates and you defect, he gets the suckers payoff. If he defects and you cooperate ....

You can see, I think, that both of you will defect again. You want to do the deal, you can smell the burgers, but there is something about the structure of the situation that keeps the deal from happening. That's why it's called a dilemma. It's called the prisoner's dilemma, by the way, because the problem was originally formulated in terms of prisoners either ratting or not ratting on their criminal friends.

Once you understand the structure of the prisoner's dilemma, you see it everywhere. Suppose you have a tofu factory that discharges ugly, toxic crud. Should you pay money to clean it up? Let's think about it. Your competitors have the same crud coming out of their factories. If they don't pay to clean up their crud and you do pay to clean up yours, you are going to have to charge more for your tofu. If you charge more than your competitors, no one will buy your tofu and you will go out of business. And besides, your small contribution to the cruddy air and water is barely significant. If you pay to clean up your crud and your competitors don't, you go out of business and the air and water are still just as cruddy. That couldn't be right.

Take the other case. You look around and see that all your competitors do clean up their crud. The air and water are pristine. In that case, hardly anyone will notice if you discharge a little crud. The air and water will be affected only imperceptibly, and you will be able to sell your tofu for less. That will enable you to drive your competitors out of business. And that will be good because you will use your money for the Good of Humankind.

The same reasoning applies if we're talking about paying your taxes or putting money in the hat for bagels at the meeting of your cheeseburger 12-step group. The temptation to defect (to "free ride" in the social dilemma case) is immense.

For simplicity of analysis, let's go back to the prisoner's dilemma. We understand the problem, and we've got some vocabulary: cooperate, defect, sucker's payoff. Now let's see what happens if we change the facts and have the players meet repeatedly. This is called an **iterated prisoner's dilemma**. If I know I'm going to be playing the cheeseburger game many times with the same opponent, what strategy would be best?

This was the question posed by Robert Axelrod at the University of Michigan and solved in a famous contest. Axelrod asked scholars all over the world to write computer programs that would play iterated prisoner's dilemma games in a round robin tournament. Every program would play against every other program, against itself, and against an opponent who cooperated and defected at random.

The winner was the shortest entry in the contest, a program that required only a few lines of code, called **Tit for Tat ("TFT")**. Its rules couldn't be much simpler. TFT always cooperates on the first move. On every subsequent move, it does what its opponent did on the previous move. Interestingly, although TFT won the tournament, it never won a single game. It never did better than tie. But when it loses, it doesn't lose by much. In a round robin tournament, where every program played against every other program and total points determined the winner, TFT came out on top.

The tournament drew a lot of attention in game theory and computer science circles and was repeated some years later with a larger field of entrants. TFT won again and has since generated a vast amount of scholarship. Boiling down the features that make TFT successful, we can identify these. It is **nice**. "Nice" is a technical term in this context. A nice program is one that is never the first to defect. In anthropomorphic terms, it gives its opponents the benefit of the doubt. It cooperates on the first move and will continue to cooperate as long as its opponent does. It is not looking for an opportunity to stick you one.

It is, however, not a patsy. It is **provocable**. It doesn't continue to cooperate when its cooperation is not reciprocated. It punishes defectors immediately. But it punishes them proportionately. If an opponent defects once, TFT defects once. If an opponent defects twice, TFT defects twice. It doesn't try to sneak in a little extra punishment. In exactly the same way that it is instantly provocable, it is instantly forgiving. As soon as TFT sees cooperation, it responds with cooperation.

It doesn't concern itself with the fact that its opponent may be slightly ahead. It doesn't care about its opponent's score. It is concerned only with its own score. It is not envious.

Finally, TFT is very easy to understand. Any program capable of learning anything can figure out what it takes to get along with TFT. Nice, provocable, forgiving, not envious, and simple. TFT gives us a winning strategy for iterated prisoner's dilemma games and a guide to lots of other behaviors in many other arenas as well. It works for training horses, for example. It also accounts, according to some scholars, for the evolution of cooperation, the title of Axelrod's magnum opus. (See also Carl Zimmer, "In Games, an Insight Into the Rules of Evolution," *New York Times*, July 31, 2007.)

There is a vast technical, and therefore largely unreadable, literature on the subject of game theory in general and the prisoner's dilemma in particular. Among the more accessible books is *Prisoner's Dilemma* by William Poundstone (which, in addition to being an introduction to game theory, is also a biography of the genius John von Neumann). For a provocative discussion of the application of game theory ideas in the real world, see James Miller, *Game Theory at Work*. And for the seminal piece on the prisoner's dilemma in negotiation, see "The Negotiator's Dilemma: Creating and Claiming Value," in Lax and Sebenius, *The Manager as Negotiator* (1986).

Tit for Tat gives us a general guide for navigating what I called the central tension in negotiation a few pages back. What is the proper mix of cooperation and competition? How do I ensure that I find the ZOPA if there is one and waste as little time as possible if there isn't? How can I share sufficient information to enable the parties to identify and explore solutions that offer maximum mutual gains on one hand, and protect information that could be exploited by my opponent on the other? The answer is to be nice, provocable, forgiving, not envious, and simple.

Start out by giving your opponent the benefit of the doubt. Assume he is interested in an honest process and a fair result. Offer a piece of information. If he reciprocates with a disclosure of his own, offer another. If he does not reciprocate, do not offer any more information until he does. In game theory language, reward cooperation and punish defection. Do so immediately and unambiguously, but do it proportionately. Make your negotiation behavior as easy as possible to understand. Your opponent should have no doubt about what it will take to get you to cooperate. Finally, measure your success against what was achievable starting where you started and given what you had. Measuring your success against your opponent's is a mistake. Remember, TFT wins tournaments over and over without winning any games, without trying to catch up to its opponents. It wins by racking up points.

This is not easy advice to take. I do a prisoner's dilemma simulation with my students every semester. Each team is assigned to act as the board of directors of a company and to set the price it will charge for its product for the following month. Both teams are provided with a payoff matrix showing the profits for each company depending on where each team sets its price. In each round the two companies set their prices simultaneously and learn what their profit will be for that month based on what they both have done. Every time I do the simulation I instruct the teams that their goal is to make as much money as they can. Pay no attention to the amount of money your opponent is making, I say. You are not going to drive them out of business. You are not trying to beat the other team. You are trying to make as much money as you can. The instructions and the payoff matrix are available in Goldberg, Sander and Rogers (1992, p. 85).

Without fail, my students ignore my instructions. Every team keeps careful track of how much money they are making compared to the other team. In every case they believe they are winning if they are making more money than the other guys, regardless of how much more they could make with a different approach.

There is plenty of evidence that my students are not alone. What we care about is how we are doing relative to others. We would rather make 60K when others are making 50 than make 70K when others are making 80. It seems to be deeply wired into the way we think. See *Choosing the Right Pond* (Frank, 1985).

§3.03(c) Rejection Then Retreat

Once we have an understanding of the reciprocity norm (§3.03(a)) and the contrast effect (§2.02(d)), we're ready to talk about a powerful negotiation technique known as **rejection then retreat**.

Suppose I ask you to lend me $100 until next week. You decline. I say "Okay, then just make it $10." What happens?

What happens, we know from experiment, is that you are far more likely to lend me the $10 if we go through the $100 request and denial first than if we don't. Obviously, your willingness to lend me $10 should be independent of whether or not I asked for $100 a minute ago. Your willingness to lend me $10 ought to be based on whether or not you have $10 to spare and whether or not you think I'm good for it. Neither of those facts can possibly have changed in the last 30 seconds.

What has changed is that you have been set up. The contrast effect has caused the $10 request to appear small by positioning it next to a $100 request. And my move from the $100 request to the far smaller $10 request looks like a concession. I opened the negotiation with a request for $100. You declined. I made a large concession and moved to a $10 request. Since I made a large move off of my original position, the reciprocity norm tells you it is your turn to make a large move off of yours.

No fact about the world has changed. You still have exactly as much cash in your pocket as you had before, and I am still exactly as questionable a credit risk as I was before. My odds of getting the $10 out of your pocket and into mine, however, have dramatically improved.

§3.03(d) More Packaging Effects

When Williams-Sonoma offered just one model of bread making machine, they achieved one level of sales performance. Then they introduced a larger, fancier, and more expensive bread maker. The new machine did not sell well, but sales of the original machine almost doubled. Why?

As usual, the answer is in the setup. Suppose I think I might like to buy a bread-making machine. I look in the Williams-Sonoma catalog and there's a bread-making machine. I consider the pros and cons. Maybe I order it, maybe I don't. There is no prominent, compromise solution.

Now take the case where I open the catalog and there are two bread-making machines, the original one and a fancier, more expensive one. The center has shifted. I like to think of myself as a reasonable person, not too cheap, not too extravagant. I want to make a reasonable decision. And now the company has provided a convenient place for me to rest. I am interested in a bread machine or I wouldn't be looking at them in the catalogue. But I don't need the fancy, expensive machine. I can happily settle for the original one.

Again, nothing has changed in the real world. The bread machine is exactly what it was, and I am exactly who I was. But in the first case I compared buying a bread machine with not buying one. In the second case the comparison is between buying the fancy one, buying the original one, and not buying one at all. The compromise choice for the reasonable guy like me is obvious.

The fancy, expensive machine is not in the catalog because Williams-Sonoma believes there is a huge demand for fancy, expensive bread machines. Of course, they are happy to sell them to people who want them. But the real reason they are in the catalog is to set up the contrast effect, to make the original machine look relatively inexpensive.

Here is a related thought experiment adapted from Thaler (1992, p. 31). Suppose you have been hanging out at the beach all day eating pretzels. Your mind is filled with the thought of how wonderful a cold Heineken would be right now. Your friend announces she is going to the run-down, dumpy looking convenience store across the street, and asks if she can bring you back anything. A beer, perhaps. You ask for a cold Heineken. She asks how much you will be willing to pay for it. What is the maximum amount you would agree to pay the convenience store for a cold beer?

Second case, same setup. You're on the beach dreaming of cold beer. Your friend announces she is going across the street to the fancy, upscale luxury hotel and will bring you back a cold one if you like. How much are you willing to pay the luxury hotel for a cold beer?

My guess is that you were willing to pay more in the second case. Why?

You know that things in fancy hotels are expensive and things in run-down convenience stores are relatively cheap. You are willing to make an allowance for that, and you expect the hotel to ask for more than the convenience store. That's fine. But notice that this has nothing to do with *you.* As in the other cases we have been discussing, nothing has changed in the real world as far as you are concerned. You are still exactly the same thirsty, sweaty person you were in the first example. The Heineken is exactly the same Heineken at the same temperature and will taste exactly the same in both cases. You're not the one going to the hotel, so you will not derive any value from the marble lobby or the air conditioning. The value of the beer from your point of view is the same in both cases. It shouldn't make any difference to you where it comes from.

I often encounter resistance when I try to explain this to students. They tell me they just don't want to get ripped off. Ten bucks for a beer from a crummy joint is a rip-off. Ten bucks for a beer from a fancy joint is par for the course. I understand that, but it's beside the point. The experience from the point of view of the beer drinker is exactly the same in either case, but in one condition he objects to the price and in the other condition he doesn't. Where we find that situation — two different reactions to the same experience — there is something to be learned.

Note the similarity between this thought experiment and the one about saving money on a purchase by walking two blocks. In that case as in this one, we were tempted to make what I would call an irrational decision because of a flaw in the decision-making process. We based our analysis on the price of the purchase rather than the amount of the savings in the first case, and we base it on the source of the beer rather than the value of the experience of drinking it in the second. There is no difference between the $25 savings on one purchase and the $25 savings on the other, but there is a change in the willingness to walk two blocks to achieve it. There is no difference between the cold beer from one source and the cold beer from the other, but there is a change in our willingness to pay for it.

The same thing — a cold beer, a two-block walk — can be perceived as more or less valuable depending on the circumstances, and the perception of that value is governed by rules. There is no more important point for negotiators. The negotiator who understands those rules has a clear and unmistakable advantage over the negotiator who does not.

The psychologically savvy negotiator is careful about the positioning of his offers. When he makes an offer, EN knows what the offer will be compared to. He is careful to position his offers where they will be perceived favorably due to the contrast effect. He is aware of where the negotiation is in terms of reciprocal concessions, and he's careful to place his offers where they will be perceived to require a reciprocal response.

§3.03(e) Choices

Sendhil Mullainathan, a Harvard professor and MacArthur genius, did a fascinating experiment in South Africa. He was working with a bank that, like other banks, wanted to make more loans. The bank sent out letters to 70,000 previous borrowers encouraging them to apply for loans. In order to see which features of the letters generated the most responses, they randomized several features of the letters. Some offered low interest rates, some high rates, some had a complicated graphic, some a simple one, some included a chance to win a cell phone, some had a picture of a bank employee that varied by race and by gender, others had a deadline. Then they carefully clocked the responses and crunched the numbers.

> What we found stunned me. We found that any one of these things had an effect equal to one to five percentage points of interest! A woman's photo instead of a man's increased demand among men by as much as dropping the interest rate five points! ... The photo, cell phone lottery, simple or complicated table, and deadline all had effects on loan applications comparable to interest. Interest rate may not even be the *third* most important factor. As an economist, even when you think psychology is important, you don't think it's *this* important. (Quoted in Lambert, 2006)

What can explain this kind of decision making?

> People are not responding to the *actual objects* they are choosing between. There is no direct relation of stimulus and response. Neoclassical economics posits a direct relationship between the object and the choice made. But in behavioral economics, the choice depends on *how the decision-maker describes the object to himself.* Any psychologist knows this, but it is revolutionary when imported into economics. (Eric Wanner, quoted in Lambert, 2006)

In other words, it isn't enough to present people with information. The information has to be presented in a way that will work with rather than against the natural grain of human information processing.

Mullainathan is working on it. He is one of the decision-making experts pioneering the field of "libertarian paternalism." He and his colleagues are looking for ways to encourage people to make decisions that they acknowledge would benefit them but that they currently are not making. The simplest example is participation in matching 401(K) plans. Participation in an employer plan that matches 401(K) contributions is like finding money in the street — especially for people who are old enough to withdraw money from the plan. The *Homo economicus* model would predict that people who were informed about simple steps they could take to get free money would be eager to take those steps. But it is not so. Not nearly as many people participate as one would expect. People, as we have seen, tend to adopt the status quo option. We choose to do nothing rather than take the time and make the effort to fill out the form and sign up even for free money. The libertarian paternalistic solution is to make these plans opt-out rather than opt-in. If we change the default option so that people who do nothing automatically Participate rather than automatically Don't Participate, we can benefit people who are subject to the status quo bias. They will never quite get around to filling out the form to opt out; they will accumulate money in the plan; and when they retire they won't have to eat cat food in the dark.

The effective negotiator is aware of the status quo bias and takes pains to choreograph choices so the default option is the desired option.

* * *

People like to have choices. Choices allow us to feel we are participating in the process, and they improve our satisfaction with the outcome. Because EN wants his negotiation opponents to feel free and happy, he gives them choices.

The opposite strategy is called **Boulwarism**. During the Cold War, Lemuel Ricketts Boulware was the vice-president of employee relations at General Electric. Boulware saw labor unions as the thin end of the wedge threatening to force the United States into socialism or worse. As a result, he believed it was important never to let the GE unions appear to have won anything at the bargaining table. He pursued a negotiation strategy that came to be named after him. Management would prepare a new contract and the union could take it or leave it. Period.

If your goal is to demoralize and defeat your negotiation opponent because of an overriding ideological commitment, perhaps Boulwarism is an appropriate strategy. If your goal is to get the most favorable outcome you can out of a negotiation, it is not. As we saw with the ultimatum game experiments in §1.01, people will sacrifice their own gain in order to punish those who are perceived as defectors. Fairness is a central element in the perception of value. And I am likely to perceive a negotiation outcome as fair in proportion to the degree to which I participated in fashioning it.

Back before belief in the unregulated free market took over American thinking, it was widely perceived that high-pressure salesmen were a problem. Fast-talking door-to-door pitchmen were selling vastly overpriced vacuum cleaners and similar items on outrageous terms and taking advantage of naïve consumers. The answer was taken to be consumer protection statutes that allowed the customer a cooling-off period during which he could rescind the transaction. Many people came to their senses after the salesman left and rescinded the agreement. Sales of overpriced vacuum cleaners plummeted.

In the continuing co-evolution of predator and prey that makes up the history of American business, the door-to-door sales companies needed a response. As Cialdini tells it, the companies' response was to increase the customer participation in fashioning the agreement. The simple expedient was to change the physical nature of the commitment. Instead of the salesman filling out the order form, the customer was asked to fill it out himself. The number of contract rescissions went down and sales returned to pre-statute levels (Cialdini, 1993, p. 79).

We talked before about the increased commitment that comes about when we write things down. Evidently this is also true of other physical actions. This is one explanation of why entry forms from Publishers Clearinghouse and similar sweepstakes involve all that tearing and pasting, licking and folding. It certainly isn't necessary to go through all that to order a magazine. Publishers Clearinghouse knows that the more physical actions we go through in sealing a deal, the more committed to that deal we become. (The power of such "involvement devices" is related to the observation that we learn something better the more of our senses we engage in learning it.) Essentially the same technique for encouraging people to follow through on their magazine subscriptions can be used to encourage people to follow through with the commitments they make in negotiation. Increase the number of ways and the kinds of ways they participate in fashioning the deal and you increase their commitment to the outcome. People follow through with their commitments when they take ownership of the process that generates them.

* * *

A second reason to give your negotiation opponent choices among alternatives is that his choices provide you with information. A cagey opponent is not likely to reveal that he has a cash-flow problem and is willing to pay a premium in exchange for favorable payment terms. But if you offer several packages of price and terms, and allow him to select from among them, you may be able to gather this helpful bit of information from a review of his choices.

§3.03(f) Reactive Devaluation

Very often people feel that their negotiation opponent is their enemy. If my opponent is my enemy, what is good for my opponent is bad for me. If my opponent makes a proposal, it must be because he would like me to accept it. But if what is good for him is bad for me, then I shouldn't accept it. Therefore, if my opponent makes a proposal, I shouldn't accept it. This line of thought presents a problem and, naturally, it has a name. It is called **reactive devaluation**.

Reactive devaluation is usually explained with reference to another concept called **fixed-pie perception**. This is the idea that the totality of benefits to be distributed among participants in the negotiation is like a pie, and that the pie cannot be enlarged. Every piece my opponent gets is a piece I don't get. The game theorists' term for this scenario is **zero-sum**. Every time I win (+1 for me), you lose (-1 for you), and vice versa. Since every +1 is paired with a -1, the game total is always 0.

This win-lose scenario was certainly prevalent in the scarcity environment of our hunter-gatherer ancestors. If you eat the rabbit,

I don't. But our world is more complicated. The pie is sometimes fixed, but not as often as we tend to think. Even in the case of a one-time sales transaction — with no continuing relationship between the parties, no reputational concerns at stake for either of the negotiators, and no linkage to future negotiations — there may still be an opportunity to trade off issues of more value to one party in exchange for issues of more value to the other. We just saw an example of this in the case of the buyer with the cash-flow problem. He was willing to pay a premium price in exchange for favorable payment terms. If the seller does not have a similar cash problem, the trade-off can benefit both parties. If the seller has an incentive to defer receipt of the payment into the next tax year, the sum total of mutual benefit may increase further.

The fixed pie perception is an illusion. It is vestigial thinking from the ancestral environment. The current fascination with **mutual-gains bargaining** is not some hippie notion about being nice to each other. It is a rational approach to getting more stuff for you and your client.

Suppose there are six apples and six oranges to be divided between us. The solution that immediately presents itself, the prominent solution, is to split them down the middle. You get three apples and three oranges; I get three apples and three oranges. No one can argue with that.

But suppose I like oranges more than I like apples. If you like apples just as well as oranges, I'll trade you one of my apples for one of your oranges and we get a deal that makes me happier without making you sadder. If you like apples more than you like oranges, we can make a deal that makes us both happier.

Fixed-pie perception leads me to believe that your valuations are the same as mine. I assume that if I like oranges better than apples, so do you. I assume further that if I were to tell you that I like oranges better than apples, you would use that knowledge against me. You would squeeze me to get more payment for the oranges. (Sorry.) So I withhold that information. Out of concern that you will use my preferences to take advantage of me, I fail to reveal them. And I wind up with a bunch of apples I don't want.

Worse, I may even misread an offer from you. If I view the negotiation as fixed-pie and I view you as sharing my valuations, how would I view an offer from you to give me more oranges in exchange for more apples? I would view it as a trick. For a fuller discussion of this problem, see *Barriers to Conflict Resolution* (Arrow et al., 1995).

It is time to get away from these fruity examples and talk about something more serious. Let's take nuclear war. Here is Congressman Floyd Spence of South Carolina talking about the Strategic Arms Limitation Talks (SALT):

> I have had a philosophy for some time in regard to SALT, and it goes like this: The Russians will not accept a SALT treaty that is not in their interest, and it seems to me that if it is in their interest, it can't be in our best interest. (Quoted in Bazerman & Neale, 1992, p. 19)

This is as clear an example of reactive devaluation as I have ever seen. It is a measure of the power of this illusion that the good Congressman was willing to risk nuclear destruction rather than call the principle into question.

> *Your proposition may be good,*
>
> *but let's have one thing understood —*
>
> *whatever it is, I'm against it!*
>
> *And even when you've changed it or condensed it,*
>
> *I'm against it!*
>
> Marx Brothers, *Horse Feathers,* 1932

Perhaps following Groucho's example, Chairman Mao said in 1939, "We should support whatever the enemy opposes and oppose whatever the enemy supports."

Here's a more current example of reactive devaluation. One of the members of the Michigan Employment Relations Commission told me recently about a collective bargaining negotiation he was once involved in. The employer proposed a four-day week. The union told him in private, "We want it, but we're afraid it might be good for the company."

Reactive devaluation is abroad in the land; there can be no question about it. Especially in negotiations with a high degree of associated emotion — family disputes, for example — there is a strong tendency to view any proposal from the other side as a trick. The logic is simple. My opponent is an SOB. He will propose something only if it benefits him. The pie over which we are negotiating is fixed, so anything that benefits him must harm me. Since any offer he proposes will really be for his own benefit and must therefore harm me (even if I can't see how), I must reject the offer.

The classic reactive devaluation experiment was performed when there was still apartheid in South Africa. At the time there was considerable controversy on American college campuses about universities divesting their holdings in companies that did business with the apartheid regime. Students were presented with two divestiture proposals. One was marked as the proposal recommended by the University's Board. The students were asked to read the proposals and say which they preferred.

It didn't matter which proposal the Board preferred; the students preferred the other one. The study has been repeated countless times. Label two proposals Democratic and Republican, and subjects will support one and oppose the other depending on their party identification. Leave the proposals in place and switch the labels, and you switch the results (Ross, 1995).

Certainly negotiations do have a distributive component — a sense in which more for your opponent means less for you. But that is not their only component. Presumably, you are involved in negotiations with this opponent in the first place because he has something you want and you don't know where you can get it elsewhere on more favorable terms. You are in this negotiation because you believe it has the potential to be better for you than your BATNA. For the same reason, your opponent is involved because he believes reaching an agreement with you could be better than *his* BATNA. In other words, every negotiation that takes place is an opportunity for both parties to improve their circumstances. If it weren't, the negotiation wouldn't take place. Your negotiation opponent is not your enemy. He is in a position to give you something you want.

As G. Richard Shell puts it, "*All deals that close are win-win deals.* The two sides would not agree to a proposal unless they thought agreement was better for them than no deal." (Shell, 1999, p. xii. Italics in original.) If a proposed settlement isn't an improvement over the status quo, or if you have a better alternative away from the table, you don't settle. You may not like dealing with your ex-spouse. You may not like the alternatives with which you are presented. Can't help you there. A successful negotiation is one where you get the best deal you can get. It is not one where you get the best deal you can imagine.

Time for another joke. *Russian guy goes to the grocer and asks the price of potatoes. The grocer says five kopeks a kilo. Guy says, "Five kopeks a kilo! Across the street they're only three kopeks a kilo." Grocer says, "So go buy them across the street." Guy says, "He's out of them right now." Grocer says, "When I'm out of potatoes, mine are only three kopeks too."*

* * *

I should mention that there is a psychological problem when we are presented with too many choices. If choices represent freedom, and freedom is good, then it's tempting to see greater choice as a greater good. This is true up to a point, but then the sheer number of available alternatives becomes overwhelming and we become paralyzed. This is the point of a book by Barry Schwartz called *The Paradox of Choice* (2004).

The best-known experiment that showed this effect involved jam. Experimenters set up a table in an upscale food store and offered free taste samples of fancy jams. In one test there were six varieties of jam available for tasting, and in the other test there were twenty-four. In both cases customers were given a dollar off a jar if they chose to buy one, and in both cases all twenty-four varieties were available.

It turned out that 30 percent of the people presented with the array of six jams bought a jar. But only 3 percent of the people presented with the full 24-variety array bought one. Schwartz's book is a good place to find a detailed exploration of this phenomenon (and much more besides). Here I will stress only that too many alternatives can make choosing difficult — and when choices are difficult, the tendency is to duck them. Being aware of this tendency, EN avoids overwhelming his opponent with too many alternative offers;

instead he offers just enough varied alternatives to ensure his opponent (a) feels he is participating and (b) reveals useful information by his choices.

§3.03(g) Finding What We Are Looking For

Another anomaly in the way people make choices is important to the negotiator who is presenting choices to an opponent. Surprisingly, we tend to make different choices among alternatives depending on whether we arrive at our choice through a process of selection or a process of exclusion. Our choice, as theorists say, is not procedure invariant. Here's an example.

Suppose you are a college student deciding where to spend your spring break. You have two reasonably priced choices:

A	B
Average weather	Lots of sunshine
Average beaches	Gorgeous beaches
Medium-quality hotel	Ultramodern hotel
Medium-temperature water	Very cold water
Average nightlife	Very strong winds
	No nightlife

Second case, same setup. Only this time you already have reservations at both places and you have to decide which reservation to cancel.

Obviously, you are making the same decision in both cases: Where are you going to spend your vacation? But the answers were not the same when the experiment was done. More people decided to go to Spot B when they were selecting than when they were arriving at the decision by a process of exclusion (Belsky & Gilovich, p. 58).

A similar effect was observed in an experiment where subjects were asked which of two parents should get custody of the children in a divorce. The parent about whom subjects were given the most information, both positive and negative, was chosen more often than the other parent both to be awarded custody and to be denied it (Thompson, p. 99).

What is going on here? It appears that in processing information we tend to find what we are looking for. In both experiments there was an "enriched" option — one where subjects were presented with a lot of information, both positive and negative — and an "impoverished" option where there was little information. When subjects were asked to select an option, they were able to find plenty of reasons to select A. When they were asked to reject an option they were also able to find plenty of reasons to reject A.

So, here is something else EN is careful about. He is aware of which of the choices he presents to his opponent is the more enriched and he poses the question in terms of selection or rejection depending on the preferred outcome. Conversely, when presented with alternatives and asked to select, EN also determines whether he would make the same decision if he had been asked to reject. If so, he knows his decision is being driven by the packaging and reconsiders.

* * *

We find what we are looking for. People who are asked if they are happy with their social life report more satisfaction than people who are asked if they are unhappy with their social life. You might want to think about that for a second.

What seems to be happening is that we consider the question by searching for confirmatory evidence. Asked if we are unhappy, we look for confirmatory evidence that we are unhappy. And there it is.

Cordelia Fine calls this the "positive test strategy" and warns, "The positive test strategy is ... why you should never, ever, ask someone you want to stay with, 'Don't you love me anymore?'" (Fine, 2006, p. 82)

§3.03(h) Loss Aversion And Framing Effects

Suppose I magically appear in the room where you are reading this book and make you the following proposal. I will flip a coin and let you call heads or tails. If you're right, I'll give you $100. If you're wrong, you give me $100. Will you take the bet? (Assume for purposes of this discussion that we are not talking about bets you can't afford to lose. It never makes sense to bet the farm.)

Let's suppose you said no. So I sweeten the deal. If you win I'll give you $125; if you lose you give me $100. Still no?

How about $150? $175?

It turns out most people won't take the bet until the payoff for winning is twice the penalty for losing.

Why should this be so? The odds of winning a coin flip are 50/50. The way to determine the value of a probability is to multiply the odds by the payoff. Using the old *Homo economicus* model of decision making, we should be willing to accept any bet where the odds times the payoff is greater than the bet. The value of a 50 percent chance of winning $150 is $75. The dis-value of a 50 percent chance of losing $100 is only $50. You should be willing to take bets like that all day.

But, once again, people do not behave according to the predictions of classical economics. The literature calls it "loss aversion." Losers cry, it is said, louder than winners sing. A gain of $150 does not make us as happy as a loss of $100 makes us sad. The economic facts are overcome by the psychological facts.

Resorting once again to evolutionary psychology, we can speculate that people had very few things in the ancestral environment, so it was important to place a high value on what we did have. A bird in the hand and all that. If all you have in the world is a stone ax, you want to be very careful about losing it.

This has a close relationship to the endowment effect (§2.01(e)), as well to concepts of sunk costs and irrational escalation of commitment (*see* §3.03(p) and (q), respectively). We cherish whatever we call ours, hold onto losing investments, and remain committed to worthless projects (including unwinnable wars) because we are reluctant to admit mistakes and because we hate to book a loss.

Evidence from the science of neuro-economics, which uses brain imaging techniques to observe the flow of oxygen in the brain as we make economic decisions — shows that loss-averse decisions engage the limbic system, an older part of the brain notably including the amygdala. By contrast, purely rational decision-making lights up more recently evolved regions, in the brain cortex (Henderson,

2006). For a book-length and very readable discussion of this topic, see *Your Money and Your Brain: How the new science of neuroeconomics can help make you rich*, by Jason Zweig (2007).

For those who prefer neurochemistry to neurophysiology, it is interesting to note that the results in neuro-economics experiments can be dramatically changed if subjects first spray Syntocinon® up their noses. Syntocinon mimics oxytocin, the "cuddle hormone." It's the one released when mothers breastfeed and when we have sex. It also produces more trust in subjects playing economic games (Cassidy, 2006).

* * *

Let's take a slightly more complicated case. I will give you a choice between A or B. If you choose A, I will promptly hand you $20. If you choose B, I will flip a coin and you will call heads or tails. If you win the flip, I will give you $40. If you lose, I will give you nothing. Which would you choose?

A. Take the $20.

B. Flip: double or nothing.

Next case. I offer you a choice (which we'll assume you cannot just reject). Choose A, you must pay me $20. Choose B, I flip a coin, you call heads or tails. If you win, you owe me nothing. If you lose, you owe me $40. Which would you choose?

A. Pay the $20.

B. Flip: double or nothing.

Again, classical economics provides a theory and a prediction. It says that you have a certain level of risk tolerance. Either you like to take a gamble or you don't. Since $20 is $20 whether you gain it or you lose it, the classical answer is that whichever choice you make — to flip or not to flip — you will make it in both cases. And again it turns out this is not the way people actually behave.

* * *

Consider this case.

You are a marine property adjuster charged with minimizing the loss of cargo on three insured barges that sank yesterday off the coast of Alaska. Each barge holds $200,000 worth of cargo, which will be lost if not salvaged within 72 hours. The owner of the local marine-salvage company gives you two options, both of which will cost the same:

Plan A. This plan will save the cargo of one of the three barges, worth $200,000.

Plan B. This plan has a one-third probability of saving the cargo of all three barges, worth $600,000, but has a two-thirds probability of saving nothing.

Which plan would you chose?

What if you were presented these two plans instead?

Plan C. This plan will result in the loss of two of the three cargoes, worth $400,000.

Plan D. This plan has a two-thirds probability of resulting in the loss of all three cargoes and the entire $600,000 but has a one-third probability of losing no cargo.

When this problem was presented to groups of insurance professionals, 71 percent of those given a choice between Plan A and Plan B chose Plan A. At the same time, 80 percent of the subjects given a choice between Plan C and Plan D chose Plan D. This despite the fact that Plan A is precisely identical to Plan C and Plan B is precisely identical to Plan D (Hammond, Keeney & Raiffa, 2001).

In other words, the distorting effect of loss aversion on our decision making is not limited to real losses. The distortion takes place when we *think* in terms of gains or losses, whether there are actual gains or losses involved or not. This is called a **framing effect**.

Research findings suggest that predictable, reliable changes in decision making can be effected by changing the frame, without changing anything else. No change in the real world is necessary. This has been demonstrated innumerable times since framing effects were discovered by Daniel Kahneman and Amos Tversky in 1979.

The implications of this research are sobering. Framing-based errors are not just committed by college sophomores who are getting paid $5 to participate in experiments at their Psych Departments.

The same effect can be produced in doctors judging which vaccines to prescribe and in military officers determining which tactics to order. When the problem is expressed in terms of lives saved, the doctors and officers — just like the insurance professionals dealing with cargo saved — overwhelmingly choose the sure thing. But when presented with an equivalent situation expressed in terms of lives lost, subjects exhibit an equally strong preference for the risky alternative.

One study concerned surgery for lung cancer. Half the subjects were told that surgery would produce a 68 percent chance of living for more than one year. The other half were told that surgery would produce a 32 percent chance of dying within one year. Since a 68 percent chance of living *is* a 32 percent chance of dying, we would expect the same number of subjects to choose surgery in either formulation. And, once again, that isn't what happened when the experiment was done. Far more subjects chose surgery when it was presented in terms of the chance of living than when it was presented in terms of the chance of dying. (Kida, p. 184).

Perhaps that result can be explained by the fact that the subjects were unsophisticated. (The study population included some doctors and graduate students, but also included patients.) But in another framing experiment, when physicians were told there was a mortality rate of 7 percent within five years for a certain operation, they hesitated to recommend it to their patients. If, on the other hand, they were told the precise equivalent in the opposite frame, that the operation had a survival rate of 93 percent after five years, they were more inclined to recommend it (Piatelli-Palmarini, 1994, p. 56).

The point is, "[T]wo ways of describing a choice that are logically equivalent … are not necessarily psychologically equivalent" (Schwartz, 2007, p. 39). "Indeed," Schwartz says, "studies on the psychology of choice somewhat radically imply that we do not strictly posses preferences and values; instead we construct them in response to the questions the world asks us or the choices it presents to us." (p. 38)

The existence of **preference reversals** depending on the way a choice is posed sets up the fascinating theoretical possibility that one might construct a "money pump."

If the subject shows a strong preference for A when presented with a choice between A and B, and an equally strong preference for D when presented with a choice between C and D, and if A is equivalent to C and B is equivalent to D (all of which we just saw in the sunken cargo case), then we have the conditions to allow construction of such a pump. The subject who strongly prefers A over B ought to be willing to pay a premium to be allowed to have his choice. Fine. He pays the premium and selects A. The experimenter then points out that A is equivalent to C. The subject realizes this. Then he is presented with an opportunity to exchange his C equivalent for a D which he strongly prefers, provided that he pay a small premium. He accepts. Then the experimenter points out that his D is equivalent to B and reminds him that he has a strong preference for A when he has this choice. The experimenter, as it happens, is willing to allow him to select A, for a small premium. He does, completing the cycle, and we may begin again.

To my knowledge, no one has yet been able to construct a money pump, but the description of preference reversals along with the explanation of the pump's theoretical possibility should serve as a cautionary tale.

There is one wrinkle here that bears mentioning. As we just saw, people tend to be risk seeking when they frame the issue in terms of losses. We would rather take the risk of a large loss than accept the certainty of a small one. That is a robust finding, demonstrated over and over in the literature. But it doesn't apply when the small loss is characterized as an insurance premium. Experiments by Slovic, Fischhoff and Lichtenstein show you can get a preference reversal depending on how you ask this question:

- Which would you prefer, paying $5 for sure or taking a 1-in-1,000 risk of paying $5,000?

  Forty percent of respondents would pay the $5.

- Which would you prefer, paying an insurance premium of $5 or taking a 1-in-1,000 risk of having to pay $5,000?

  Sixty-six percent would pay the $5 (Plous, 1993, p. 52).

Because the decision to settle or to litigate a lawsuit is exactly the choice between taking the sure thing or taking a risk, this area should be of particular interest to lawyers involved in settlement discussions. I offer my suggested method for dealing with framing effects in Chapter 5.

§3.03(i) Size And Timing Of Concessions

Once the negotiation has proceeded to the point where concessions are being exchanged, EN is careful to note both the size and the timing of both his opponent's concessions and his own. As we have seen, the guy who wants the deal the worst gets the worst deal. And, as we have also seen, leverage is a matter of perception. Consequently, you do not want to be perceived as wanting the deal worse than your opponent wants it. That's why you don't want to move any faster or any farther than he moves. If you have taken care to see that the midpoint between your first offer and his is in a favorable part of the ZOPA, this procedure should get you where you want to go.

In Hollywood, I am told, producers and agents long ago figured out that delaying the response to an offer signals leverage. The party who can't find the time to reply obviously has more important things to do than worry about this deal. If you are waiting anxiously for an answer and your opponent isn't even bothering to think about it, you obviously need the deal more than he does. And if you need it more than he does, you are going to have to move farther than he will to get it to happen.

Realizing this, you call back. If you're desperate enough, you make a consecutive unreciprocated concession. Your opponent ignores that too. Perhaps you'll make another one. The deal moves all the way over to his end of the ZOPA, and all he has to do is not answer his phone.

The following dream scenario is based on an apocryphal Hollywood story that people all over California swear happened to a friend of someone their sister knows.

Phone rings.

Hollywood Producer: We love your treatment and we want to make the picture. We need you to move out here and do the screenplay right away. We'll give you $200,000.

Free-lance Writer: That's wonderful! I'm very excited. But of course I'll have to talk to my husband before I make a decision.

HP: Make it $300,000.

F-L W: Oh my, thank you very much. But I really do have to talk to my husband before …

HP: Alright, $400,000.

F-L W: Omigoodness, $400,000! But my husband …

HP: $500,000 is my final offer. Take it or leave it.

F-L W: We'll take it.

Maybe this happened, and maybe it didn't. The point is that reluctance can signal leverage.

Of course, it's never quite that simple. As already noted, there is an arms race going on. The smarter the sellers get, the wilier the buyers must become in order to survive. The more savvy the buyers get, the sneakier or smarter the sellers must become. Once it is known that reluctance signals leverage, some negotiators will exhibit false reluctance. In nature, if there are poisonous red bugs that birds have learned not to eat, evolution will produce red bugs that are not poisonous. Redness is biologically cheap. Poison is expensive. If redness keeps birds away, poison isn't necessary.

This co-evolutionary process caused Hollywood types to raise ignoring each other to an art form. I am told that during the '80s it was common for parties, even if both were eager to get a deal, to refuse to return one another's calls for weeks. Eventually, of course, this strategy gets "solved." At this point, my sources tell me, the interpretation has flipped: The longer they delay, the *more* they want the deal.

This is a murky area. Perhaps the only advice is to be aware of it. If you move faster or farther than your opponent, you may want to say why. "I am going to make a substantial move here because I am a very busy guy with plenty of other things to do, and I don't have time to chip away at this deal $1,000 at a time." This kind of statement can permit a large move without betraying a lack of leverage.

* * *

Finally, EN is aware of the pattern of concessions. Typically, as a party approaches his reservation point, the size of his concessions will decrease. If I start at $100 and go to $80, then $70, then $68, then $67, and $66.50, you probably get the idea that my walk-away price is $65. The pattern tells you that I am not going below $65.

That may be because I actually will not go below $65, or it may be because I want you to think I won't. As I said, murky.

§3.03(j) Scarcity

We want what we can't have. There is something irresistible about forbidden fruit. It's an old story. Citizens over the legal drinking age in America have an almost infinite variety of food and drink available to them. But there is one particular white powder you must not put up your nose. What result? Billions are spent on cocaine and all of us are banished forever from the Garden of Eden.

How does this work? One explanation is that our reaction is a form of loss aversion. If I tell you there is only one more potrzebie left, and that once it is gone you will never be able to get another one, you experience a threat of loss. Your freedom to be the owner of a potrzebie is about to disappear. We all hate loss. So you buy the potrzebie.

This is, of course, the reason so many products are available "in limited quantities" and "for a limited time only." Since all earthly goods are available in limited quantity and for a limited time, these phrases do not convey any actual information. What they do is leverage the scarcity weapon.

I once heard a bluegrass musician explain how he got to be such a good picker. He said his grandfather tuned up a mandolin real good, set it in the corner and said, "You kids stay away from that mandolin."

I can no longer trace the origin of my favorite scarcity story. It concerns the purchase of a banjolele, a hybrid instrument brought about by the union of a banjo and a ukulele. It seems the narrator was poking around in a hock shop when he noticed the odd-looking object. He was examining it when the proprietor came over and said,

"You must be Ralph." The narrator said no, he was not Ralph. The proprietor explained that he had just gotten a call from Ralph. He asked if the banjolele was still available and said he was on his way over to get it. The narrator scooped up the banjolele, bought it for the price on the tag, and hurried out the door before Ralph could show up. Only later did it dawn on him that Ralph didn't exist.

Perhaps Ralph did not enjoy actual physical existence, but it is likely that the proprietor and his imaginary friend had been partners in a lucrative business for many years.

Real estate sales people are famous for the phantom offer gimmick. "There is someone else coming to look at the house later today." Some private sellers of used cars will put an ad in the paper, ask people to call for an appointment and then schedule all the appointments at the same time. If there aren't enough real potential buyers to make a small crowd, such sellers may enlist friends or relatives to stand around in the driveway looking eager.

The scarcity weapon can be over-played, of course. The phrase "limited edition" began appearing on candy packaging a few years ago. Hershey's cherry cordial kisses and Snickers® Xtreme were examples. Eventually a commentator noted that "the sheer variety of limited editions has created the odd impression of an oversupply of supposedly scarce products" (Walker, 2006).

The scarcity weapon is what drives negotiation deadlines. Anyone who has engaged in settlement discussions has heard this thinly veiled threat: "At this point my client is prepared to settle for X. But if we have to engage in expensive discovery and retain an expert and all the rest of it, the settlement price is going to go up." Sometimes this is accompanied by a time limit. "I'll keep this offer open for 24 hours. After that the offer comes off the table and we start over."

If you believe him, this may work. If you believe he would take $20,000 today but the day after tomorrow he would refuse it, he may be able to get you to offer $20,000. But why would that be so? What's the real difference between today and the day after tomorrow?

Once you begin to ask questions like this, the scarcity weapon loses some of its effectiveness. Not long ago I saw a sign by the roadside that said:

Needed
36 people to Make Money and lose 10 lbs in 14 days

Right. Better call now. If you're the 37th person, they will turn you down.

The point is that a scarcity claim has to be credible. There has to be some actual reason for a deadline or for a claim of limited availability. Otherwise it's obviously just bluster.

This brings into play another piece of packaging advice. People don't like to be threatened, but they don't mind being warned. There is a difference between saying "If you don't accept my offer today, I'm taking it off the table" and saying "Tomorrow is the end of the reservation period when the company sets its reserves for outstanding lawsuits. If I can go back with a settlement today, the settlement will come out of the current period reservation fund. But after today, the reservation funds go into the retention account for previous lawsuits and the valuation is booked based on the retention amounts in the subsequent quarter. So after today the new formula will apply and that settlement amount won't be available."

This is gibberish, of course, but it is gibberish of a specific kind. It is expressed in terms of a warning rather than a threat. I'm not telling you I'm taking the offer off the table if you don't accept today. That isn't credible. I'm telling you that vast and mysterious forces beyond my control are taking the offer off the table. I'm trying to help you out here.

Because he is aware of the problem of making threats credible, and aware of the common resistance to threats, EN prefers warnings.

§3.03(k) Commitment And Consistency

Thinking is expensive. It takes a lot of blood to run the brain, and it takes a lot of calories to circulate the blood. Thinking takes time and attention away from activities that evolution thinks are more important, like finding food, fighting off predators, and having sex. So we avoid thinking when we can. We use heuristics instead.

We can imagine that there are two piles of documents in the brain, one marked Decisions to Make, the other marked Decisions Already Made. Our preference is to move documents from the first pile into the second with as little effort as possible and not to let any documents slip back into the undecided pile once they have been decided. We are busy with new decisions. If old decisions insist on being reconsidered, the whole system will bog down. So we have a rule that says the way a decision was made the first time is the way it will be made henceforth. We agree with Friedrich Nietzsche, "It is hard enough to remember my opinions, without also remembering my reasons for them!"

Evidently, this tendency prevails even in medicine. In *How Doctors Think*, Jerome Groopman talks about a procedure to remove fluid from around a patient's heart. It's done by sticking a needle under the xiphoid, the cartilage at the lower end of the breastbone, and up toward the right collar bone through the pericardium.

"Why do you stick the needle under the xiphoid?"

"Because that was how my teachers taught me in my training."

"And why do you think your teachers taught you the way they did?"

"Because that's how they were taught."

It turns out that this old, indirect method was designed to minimize the significant danger of piercing one of the coronary arteries. Now that the fluid removal procedure is done under ultrasound guidance, the arteries can be avoided and the needle can go directly to where the fluid is (Groopman, 2007, p. 138). But in order for that change to take place, someone had to ask the question. Someone had to have the temerity to ask whether the received wisdom was so wise. It's easier not to do that. It's easier to proceed as if that question has already been answered and to trust the answer. (But see "How Doctors Think They Think" by Charles Lambdin for a well-reasoned critical review of Groopman's book; it's available at www.skeptic.com/eskeptic/07-08-22.html.)

In previous chapters we touched on the directional tendency established by first impressions and early verbal commitments. This is what Cialdini calls the commitment and consistency principle. It is the basis of the ancient sales technique called the foot-in-the-door. If I can get you to make one small purchase, you change from being a prospect to being a customer. It is easier to sell to a customer than to a prospect. And this is so because the customer has put this decision in the Decisions Already Made pile and doesn't want to have to take it out.

I don't know enough about neurophysiology to say whether there is a structure in the brain that corresponds to the Decisions Already Made pile, but the evidence for its functional existence is strong. Take this famous example.

Experimenters went door to door, asking people if they would display a three-inch sign on their house that said BE A SAFE DRIVER. Some people agreed and some people didn't. Then the experimenters went back two weeks later and asked if people would allow them to erect a billboard in their front yard that said DRIVE CAREFULLY. Among subjects who had not been offered the little sign, 83 percent declined the billboard. But among the people who had previously agreed to display the small sign, 76 percent agreed to *accept* the billboard (Cialdini, 1993, p. 72).

Because of the power of commitment and consistency, recent research has shown that car buyers loyal to one make of car pay more for their cars than first-time buyers of that make. Why? Because first-time buyers have to be persuaded, and price is one of the ways to persuade them. Loyal buyers do not need a price cut to be convinced to continue buying the same make. They need only to look in the Decisions Already Made pile and see. I drive Pontiacs. I don't have to revisit that decision every time I need a new car.

The Commitment and Consistency principle is also behind the willingness of oriental rug merchants to let you take a rug home and look at it in your house. It is behind the ingenious 24-hour test drive recently introduced by Cadillac. Once the salesman's foot is in the door, our cognitive parsimony is likely to help him get the rest of the way in.

Publicity is important here. Jurors who vote by secret ballot are more likely to be persuaded to change their minds than jurors who vote openly. Having made a public commitment, we feel we must continue to act in a manner consist with that commitment or lose face.

Back in §2.03(d) when we were talking about the schmooze, I discussed the technique of securing a commitment. "Are you ready to buy today?" the salesman asked. We didn't see any danger in agreeing. We can always change our mind. If we say "No, just looking" we won't get as much attention. Why not agree? Harmless, right? Now what Cialdini calls a **consistency trap** is springing closed. For reasons of cognitive parsimony it is easier to buy the car than backtrack on the commitment.

This is why Amazon.com suggests you put things in your shopping cart. You can always take them out later. Sure you can.

When used by a mediator, the commitment and consistency weapon can make it easier for parties to agree to settlements. One technique often used in domestic relations mediation is to seek an early commitment to a guiding principle. John and Mary are getting a divorce. They hate each other, and each seems motivated only by the desire to cause the other harm. On the table is the custody and visitation question with regard to little Emmylou. The mediator might start by talking to John about what a satisfactory settlement would look like. John says a satisfactory settlement would be one that keeps Emmylou away from Mary, since she is a Satanist and a drunk. The mediator thanks John politely and turns to Mary. What does she think a satisfactory settlement would look like? Mary says it would be one that keeps Emmylou away from John, since he is a dope fiend and a psychopath. The mediator thanks her politely and says, "While you certainly have your differences, that is to be expected under the circumstances. What pleases me is that you both agree the most important thing we are going to work to accomplish here is to reach the solution that is going to be the best for little Emmylou. Isn't that right? That's the most important thing? And we all agree?"

It is difficult for either John or Mary to disagree. Whatever they may be thinking in their treacherous and hate-filled hearts, publicly they are going to agree that all they want is what's best for Emmylou.

This sets the tone of the negotiation. Whenever the session degenerates to the Hobbesian war of all against all, the mediator can gently remind the participants of what they agreed was the goal of the mediation.

I am making two points here. One is that the commitment and consistency weapon has benign uses as well as purely self-serving ones. The larger point is that a negotiator will have an easier time getting an opponent to agree to a position when it follows from a position to which the opponent is already committed. This is not a difficult concept, but it is surprising how often it is ignored in practice.

Suppose I am trying to get you to vote for Fester Bestertester. There are two ways to do that. The hard way is first to convert you to supporting Bestertester's position on, say, tax subsidies for tofu farmers, and then to point out that Bestertester is in the forefront on that issue. The easy way is to find out where you and Bestertester agree and pound that. Tax subsidies for tofu farmers? That's Bestertester.

Yet negotiators do it the hard way all the time. They spend enormous time and effort, for example, trying to convert their opponents to seeing their lawsuit from their point of view. This is not any more likely to happen than that you are going to see your lawsuit from their point of view. That's not how people work. They tend to behave in ways that are consistent with their previous actions and previous statements. They believe in a coherent, consistent worldview. The goal of an effective negotiator is not to convert their opponents to a different worldview. It is to show the opponent that the desired settlement is a logical consequence of the worldview they already have.

This is what Bill Ury, the greatest aphorist in dispute resolution, means when he says "Let them have your way." Settlements are best — that is, they are easiest to get and most likely to be complied with — when they grow out of who your opponent is. You let them have your way when you gently help them see that your way is their way.

If my opponent is a tough, no-nonsense business type, my strategy is to show that an early settlement is a money saver. Settlement is an affirmation of a value he already holds. It is consistent with his pre-existing view of himself. If my opponent is motivated by patriotism or religiosity or family values or bead collecting, my strategy is to show how an early settlement can free up time so she can get back to what's really important. The EN takes his negotiation opponent where he finds him. He doesn't make extra work for himself by trying to change his opponent's values. He uses his opponent's values as a lever.

§3.03(l) Confirmation Bias

One reason the commitment and consistency weapon works is that, once a decision has been made, we tend to exhibit **confirmation bias**; that is, we overweight new data that support the decision and underweight new data that disconfirm it. One reason we do this is that disconfirmation requires more cognitive effort than confirmation. Another reason is that we don't like to change our mind, because we don't like to admit we made a mistake the first time.

Let's talk more about confirmation, disconfirmation, and cognitive load. The claim here is that the brain has an easier time thinking in terms of positive statements rather than negative ones. If you remember taking a class in symbolic logic, you will recall that everyone instantly understood *modus ponens*:

If P then Q

P

Therefore Q

But lots of people had difficulty grasping *modus tollens*:

If P then Q

Not Q

Therefore Not P

Modus tollens is just not as obvious. Sometimes an overload of negations can create a cognitive fire hazard, as when a court denies an appeal seeking to overturn the refusal of the lower court to dismiss the defendant appellee's motion to reconsider the earlier denial.

The difference between the cognitive load required to consider confirmation of a thesis and the cognitive load required to consider disconfirmation can be seen in the following demonstration (Plous, p. 12).

Suppose you have four cards. Each card has a number on one side and a letter on the other. They look like this:

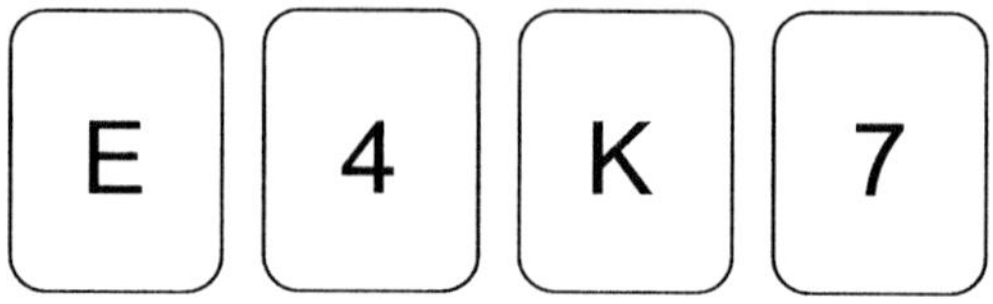

Someone tells you, "If a card has a vowel on one side, then it has an even number on the other side." You want to know whether that rule is true. Which cards would you have to turn over to find out? Think about this before you continue.

* * *

Most people understand they would have to turn over the **E** card to see if the rule is true. Many people believe they would have to turn over the **4** card. Thinking about it for a while, however, should convince you that turning over the **4** card can't help you much. If the **4** has a consonant on the other side, it doesn't matter. If the **4** has a vowel, it means the rule is confirmed in this instance, but that doesn't prove the rule is true. Proving the rule requires showing that no counterexample exists.

(Consider the classic statement "All swans are white." Finding a white swan or 10 white swans or **n** white swans doesn't prove that all swans are white. But finding a single black swan would *disprove* that statement.)

Back to our cards. What if you turn over the **K**? Nothing happens. If it has an odd number on the other side, that neither confirms nor disconfirms the rule. If it has an even number, that doesn't matter either. The rule never said that a card with an even number on one side has to have a vowel on the other. We're testing whether a card with a vowel on one side has an even number on the other. (All swans are white, not all white things are swans.)

Finally, what about the 7? If the 7 has a consonant on the other side, that has no effect on our task. But if the 7 has a vowel on the other side, that's the black swan: Then we *know* the proposed rule is false.

The correct answer to the problem, then, is as follows: To test the rule that all vowel cards have an even number on the back, you have to turn over the **E** and the **7**. This is very difficult for some people to see. And it is difficult to see because disconfirmation requires a greater cognitive load than confirmation. That's why we have a confirmation bias.

* * *

The following case, however, illustrates a fascinating exception to confirmation bias. Four people are sitting at a bar, and you want to know if any illegal underage drinking is going on. The four people look like this:

- 15-year-old girl
- 60-year-old man
- Person drinking Coke
- Person drinking gin

You can check a person by looking at their ID or by testing what's in their glass. Who would you have to check?

No one has any problem with this example. Everyone instantly and intuitively knows you need to check the 15-year-old girl and the person drinking gin, and that checking the other two would be pointless. This is fascinating because, as a few moments' reflection will show, this problem is logically identical with the preceding card problem!

Why is the card problem difficult for so many people when the identical drinking problem is perfectly obvious? The answer seems to be that one cognitive wiring system stronger than our confirmation bias is our cheater-detection system. We are, it seems, exquisitely sensitive detectors of cheating. We saw a glimpse of this when we discussed the ultimatum game in §1.01. People will hurt themselves — act against their own self interest and take money out of their own pockets — in order to teach a lesson to those who would take more than their fair share of public goods. We also saw this in §3.03(b) when we dealt with the prisoner's dilemma and related social dilemmas.

* * *

Getting back to confirmation bias: In *How Doctors Think*, Jerome Groopman discusses a phenomenon he calls **diagnosis momentum.** Once a doctor has made a diagnosis, it is not only difficult for *that* doctor to change his mind and consider other diagnoses; it is even difficult for *other* doctors to consider other diagnoses. Once a label is affixed to a patient's condition, the label tends to remain affixed. New information that does not confirm the diagnosis tends to be underweighted or ignored. Since it's been already decided that the patient has Disease X, the fact that she doesn't have the elevated blood count usually associated with Disease X must be because it is early in the course of the disease and the elevated blood count hasn't had time to develop yet.

In medicine this kind of mistake can have profoundly dangerous consequences. In law the consequences are rarely life-threatening, but the phenomenon is equally common and correspondingly dangerous.

Many times as a mediator I have watched as lawyers receive new information about their cases from their opponents. Many times, in my view, the new information has been utterly devastating to the case. But it is rare that I have seen lawyers change their minds. Part of the explanation for this is that the people I am watching are lawyers paid to represent clients. As Upton Sinclair said, "It is difficult to get a man to understand something when his salary depends upon his not understanding it." But another part of the problem, I am convinced, is what we might call evaluation momentum. A lawyer who thinks he has a winning case will continue to think so even in the face of compelling evidence to the contrary. As a result of confirmation bias, such evidence will be discounted or ignored.

* * *

Sit down with a group of friends or students and give them the series of numbers 6, 8, 10. Tell them the series conforms to a rule, and their job is to figure out what the rule is. The way they are to do this is to propose other series of three numbers. You will tell them whether their series conforms to the same rule or not.

The rule is "Any series of numbers in increasing order of magnitude."

Notice what your subjects do. Inevitably they will look at the series and notice that it contains three consecutive even numbers. They will arrive at the hypothesis that the rule is three consecutive even numbers, and they will attempt to test it by presenting three other consecutive even numbers. They will say something like 14, 16, 18 and get a yes. This will encourage them, and they will do it again.

This is diagnosis momentum together with confirmation bias. The mind fixes on a solution — a diagnosis if you are a doctor, a theory of the case if you are a lawyer, three consecutive even numbers if you're playing this game — and then looks for confirming evidence. With some audiences the game never progresses beyond this level. They propose a few series of consecutive even numbers, get a few 'yes' answers, and announce that they have solved the problem.

Negotiators, of course, are subject to the same cognitive biases as other humans. We process affirmation more easily than we process negation, and confirmation better than disconfirmation. It's hard for us to change our minds.

§3.03(m) Theory Of Mind

Try this. Think of a song — "Happy Birthday," "The Star Spangled Banner," "Mary Had a Little Lamb," something everybody knows. Find a partner and tap out the rhythm of the song on your partner's wrist.

da DUM da dum da DUM da dum …

Can he guess what song you're tapping? No? Do it again. Still no? Try a different song. Try a different partner. Tap HARDER.

What's the matter here? Isn't it perfectly obvious?!

da DUM da dum da DUM da dum da DUM da dum da DUM

o BEAU-ti-ful for SPA-cious skies / For AM-ber waves of GRAIN, …

a-MER-ri-ca! a-MER-ri-ca! / God SHED his grace on THEE …

No, it is not perfectly obvious. Or, more correctly, while it is perfectly obvious to *you*, it is likely to be perfectly opaque to your partner. You are singing "America the Beautiful" in your head. You can't *not* hear the song. Your partner is not singing "America the Beautiful" in his head.

Theory of mind is what psychologists call the awareness that different people have different ideas in their heads. It is a concept we generally expect to see developed by the time a child is a few years old. Infants don't have it. Four-year-olds do.

Suppose you and Fonebone are in a room with a toddler. Fonebone and the toddler watch you put a cookie in a box. Fonebone leaves the room. While he's gone you take the cookie out of the box and put it in your pocket. Fonebone comes back into the room. You tell Fonebone to find the cookie.

Then you ask the toddler, "Where will Fonebone look for the cookie?" At two, the kid will predict that Fonebone will look for the cookie in your pocket. He doesn't have what it takes to distinguish between what he knows and what Fonebone knows. A four-year old, by contrast, will have no problem (Sally, 2006, p. 378).

The four-year old understands that not everyone sees the world the same way he sees it. Participants in the tapping game, 18-month-old babies, designers of DVD players, and the principal parties in domestic disputes do not.

§3.03(n) Partisan Perception

Besides our tendency toward reactive devaluation, our inclination to behave consistent with our earlier statements and our confirmation bias, we tend to experience the world in a partisan way. When we like someone, we see the world in a way that is biased in their favor.

This was shown in an elegant experiment involving tennis. Subjects were introduced either to a likeable, friendly tennis player or a rude, unfriendly one. Then they were asked to watch a tennis match and call when the ball was out of bounds. Importantly, the subjects were told their calls would have no effect on the scoring of the match. They were just supposed to call 'em like they saw 'em. And what they saw was that the nice people's shots were in and the nasty people's shots were out (Fine, 2006, p. 45).

A similar thing happened in a famous experiment involving Ivy League football. A group of Dartmouth students was shown a film of a Princeton-Dartmouth game and asked to record any infractions they saw committed by either team. A group of Princeton students was shown the same film and given the same instructions. The Dartmouth students saw about as many infractions being committed by Princeton as by Dartmouth. But the Princeton students saw Dartmouth commit more than twice the number of infractions than the Princeton team. The experimenters concluded:

> It seems clear that the "game" was actually many different games .... It is inaccurate and misleading to say that different people have different "attitudes" concerning the same "thing." For the "thing" simply is not the same for different people whether the "thing" is a football game, a presidential candidate, Communism, or spinach (Hastorf and Cantril, 1954, quoted in Plous, 1993, p. 19).

To this must be added the psychological fact that we do not experience some things at all. My personal favorite demonstration of this phenomenon is another famous experiment. It involves a video clip of six people passing two basketballs. Three of the people in the clip are wearing white shirts and three are wearing black shirts. At the time of this writing the clip is available on the web at http://viscog.beckman.uiuc.edu/grafs/demos/15.html. If at all possible, watch this short video a few times before reading further. *Your assignment for the first viewing is to count the number of times the people in white shirts pass the ball to one another.*

Concentrating on counting the passes between the white shirts, roughly half the people who watch this clip fail to see a woman dressed in a full gorilla suit walk into the midst of the action, stop, pound on her chest and walk slowly off (Simons & Chabris, 1999).

* * *

To summarize: We see what we are looking for, what we expect to see, what we have seen before, what we want to see. In a dispute where money, ego, self regard, reputation and more can be at stake, it's no wonder we have difficulty agreeing on the facts, much less on the appropriate solution.

§3.03(o) Social Proof

When people don't know what to do, they look around to see what other people are doing and do that. This is what Cialdini calls **social proof**. Once again, we can see how doing what the rest of the tribe is doing was an adaptive strategy in the ancestral environment.

As a default position, doing what the rest of the tribe is doing is probably safe. If everyone is running that way as fast as they can, the odds are it's a good idea to do the same. It is probably not wise to stop to investigate and inquire or to adopt a contrarian attitude and go the other way. Sometimes, perhaps, but not often enough to be worth the risk.

This ancient inclination persists in our modern circumstances. I remember sneaking down to check out the early arrivals at my first National Academy of Arbitrators reception. Were the men wearing suits or navy blazers? I wanted to look like a member of the tribe. (The answer, by the way, was blazers for the Thursday night reception, suits for the Saturday night dinner.)

To some extent we have evolved as herd animals. If we see people running, we run. If we hear people laughing, we laugh. This is not because we consciously want to be like other people as I did at the Academy meeting. It is because the sound of people laughing makes us think what is happening is funny. We consistently judge television shows with laugh tracks funnier than shows without them.

Back in the 1950s the psychologist Solomon Asch did a famous experiment in which he asked people which of three lines was the same length as a fourth line. Anyone could plainly see what the correct answer was, but a substantial number of subjects got it wrong. They got it wrong because before they answered they heard the answers given by a number of other "subjects" who got it wrong. The other subjects were, of course, confederates of the experimenter, and the goal of the study was to measure social conformity. Some of the subjects reported that they went along with the majority even though they knew it was wrong, because they didn't want to stick out and be thought peculiar.

Others, however, reported that they really did perceive the wrong answer as right. New evidence from the nascent science of neuro-economics supplies some surprising support for this latter explanation. Evidently the brain undergoes neurological changes when we observe the behavior of other members of our tribe.

* * *

This is why sales pitches emphasize that our brand is the most popular, largest selling, fastest growing. Your internal, instinctive decision maker judges that it is in your interest to make the choice made by so many other members of the tribe and buy the same brand.

The same social proof weapon is at work when your lawyer tells you your severed leg is worth $500,000 in Wayne County, Michigan. Other people in this jurisdiction have received awards clustering around $500,000 for their severed legs. That's the going market price. You are selling yourself cheap if you accept substantially less, and you're being greedy if you demand more. The right number is 500K.

Why is it the right number? Because lots of similarly situated people have determined that it is the number they are willing to take or pay. It is deemed to be sufficient to compensate you for your injury because it has been deemed to compensate others for theirs. That's all there is to it.

At that point the burden shifts to you to show that yours was a particularly excellent leg or that your relationship to it was particularly close. Some adjustment may be appropriate in light of your peculiar circumstances, but the anchor price is the one set by the market.

This is not unreasonable. It's difficult to come up with a better approach. But I think it's important to see what is happening here and to be able to identify social proof when we see it being used.

* * *

The Meltsner and Schrag article mentioned in §2.02 includes a negotiation tip that operates on the basis of the social proof principle. They suggest you arrange for your negotiating team to slightly outnumber your opponent's. Meltsner and Schrag say it is a feature of group behavior that the solution that emerges from group decision-making tends toward the average of the positions of the members of the group. Having more members of the group who feel as you do would therefore pull the group's decision in your direction.

The members of the group look around for social clues to tell them what to do. If a majority of the people in the room support your view, they provide just the social cue you want. Note that this technique works on the members of your own team as well as your opponent's. If the members of your team find reinforcement in the majority of faces they see around the table, they are less likely to be converted to the other side's point of view.

Note also, however, that this technique has a substantial downside. If you insulate yourself from being persuaded by the arguments of your opponents — using this technique or any other — you also reduce the chance that you will be corrected when you are wrong. This is the danger called **groupthink**.

The word groupthink was made famous by Yale psychologist Irving Janis. He was trying to understand how so many smart people in the Kennedy administration could have agreed on something as obviously stupid as the Bay of Pigs invasion. He determined that bloody fiasco and others came about as a result of:

> a mode of thinking that people engage in when they are deeply involved in a cohesive in-group, when the members' strivings for unanimity override their motivation to realistically appraise alternative courses of action .... Groupthink refers to a deterioration of mental efficiency, reality testing, and moral judgment that results from in-group pressures. (Janis, 1972, p. 9)

Two decision-making tools are recommended to avoid groupthink. One is to see to it that decision-making groups are diverse. This is good news for proponents of a more inclusive workplace. Diversity in hiring and promotion is justified not just on the basis of fairness and political correctness. Diverse decision-making groups make demonstrably better decisions. And the more diverse, the better. I am not saying that your negotiation team should express its diverse points of view at the bargaining table. At the table it is best to speak with one voice. I'm suggesting that back in the privacy of your own team's deliberations it is best if different views are encouraged.

The other tool is the Catholic Church's old idea of the Devil's Advocate. Back in the 16th century, the Church developed the practice of appointing a clerical official to oppose the canonization of any proposed new saint. This person was given the tools he needed to test and probe and look for holes and errors in the accounts favoring sainthood. It is a radical concept and one that shows a deep intuitive understanding of the mistakes to which decision-making groups are prone. Groups as well as individuals are prone to confirmation bias, the tendency to overweight new information that confirms earlier impressions and to underweight disconfirmatory evidence. The idea of appointing a respected official to publicly challenge the evidence brought forth in support of canonization was an impressive bit of leadership. (The practice was officially discontinued by Pope John Paul II.)

Unfortunately, the Devil's Advocate idea is unlikely to gain much traction in the world of politics or business, or in our personal lives. This is the inverse of the similarity-attraction effect we discussed in 2.03(b). The people who make the best Devil's Advocates are probably going to be people we don't like (Russo & Shoemaker, 1990, p. 45).

§3.03(p) Sunk Costs

The **sunk cost fallacy** is the erroneous belief that somehow past costs can be redeemed by future ones. For many years I taught the sunk cost fallacy to my students using the Vietnam War as an example. U.S. decision makers felt they had to continue to send soldiers to die in Vietnam because if they didn't, the soldiers they sent previously would have died in vain. As I have gotten older and my students have gotten younger, the Vietnam experience has faded into history and no longer resonates with them. In August of 2005 President Bush provided a fresh example. Speaking of the (then) nearly 2,000 Americans who had died in Iraq, he said "We owe them something. We will finish the task that they gave their lives for."

There may be sound reasons to continue to pursue the war in Iraq. I don't personally happen to think so, but that is not the point. The point is that the fact that many soldiers have died in pursuit of a policy, any policy, *cannot* be a reason to continue it. Past losses can never be the justification for future actions. But we persist in feeling that they can.

We think, "We can't kill that program, sell that stock, end that war. We've got too much invested in it!"

The point is, the money you have invested is gone whether you kill the program or not. The future of the program or the investment or the war should depend only on your best judgment of its future, not on its cost in the past.

The sunk cost fallacy is also a factor in many other spheres of activity. For example:

> [P]rofessional basketball coaches give more playing time to players earning higher salaries, independent of their current level of performance. And people who have started their own businesses are more likely to invest in expanding them than people who have purchased their businesses from others. (Schwartz, 2004, p. 161).

Similarly: "The fact that no major dam in the United States has been left unfinished once begun shows how far a little concrete can go in defining a problem" (Fischhoff et al., 1981, quoted in Plous, 1993, p. 244).

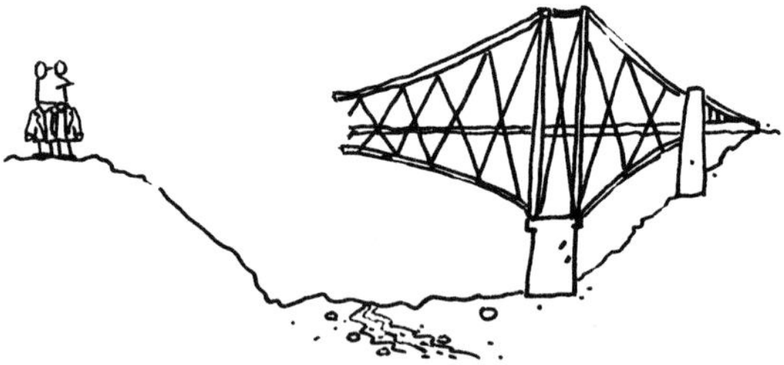

Here's my personal favorite sunk cost experiment. Suppose you buy a frozen dinner on sale for $5.00. You come home. You call up a friend to see if she would like to come over and eat frozen dinner too. She says yes. You go out to buy another dinner, but they are no longer on sale and you have to pay the full price of $10.00. You come home and cook both dinners. Phone rings. It's your friend and she's not coming. You can't eat both dinners. You can't freeze one. It's too late to call anyone else. Which dinner do you eat, the one that cost $5 or the identical one that cost $10? (Belsky & Gilovich, 1999, p. 67)

I particularly like this example because it's easy to see both points. It is absolutely pointless to distinguish between the two dinners. They are identical. The money is spent and cannot be recovered no matter which dinner you eat. And, at the same time, it's harder to throw away a perfectly good dinner for which you paid $10 than it is to throw away an identical dinner for which you paid $5.

It shouldn't matter how much you paid for your basketball player, your hydro-electric dam, or your war. The money you paid is gone no matter what you do. Yet in experiment after experiment, project after project, war after war, we keep believing it makes a difference.

We can try to overcome this problem, or we can use it. If you are trying to lose weight, you can buy an expensive health club membership. Because of the sunk cost fallacy you will have the feeling you wasted your money unless you use the club.

You can do a thought experiment to measure this effect. Suppose you followed my weight loss advice and bought an expensive six-month health club membership. Now suppose an identical club opened up the same distance away and offered a free membership for six months. Which one would you go to? Now move the free club closer. Same answer? Now make it a little better. Then make it a lot better. Same answer? Can you justify your choices? When are you going to stop going to the less convenient, lower quality facility? The answer to that question is a measure of the force of the sunk cost fallacy.

The money you spent on your membership is spent. It's sunk. It's gone and nothing can bring it back. Continuing to go to the crummy joint *cannot* make sense.

It is a robust effect, however, and you *can* use it on your negotiation opponents. An offer that did not look good early in a long negotiation can begin to look better later on, by force of the sunk cost fallacy. At 9:00 in the morning that offer would have caused him to leave and waste no further time. Now that it's 5:00 in the evening and he has spent the whole day at the table, walking away is more difficult. It means he has to admit he wasted the day. The sunk cost fallacy urges him to salvage something out of the day and take the deal.

§3.03(q) Escalation Of Commitment

The negotiator who is fooled by the sunk cost fallacy can also be encouraged to increase his bet. This goes by the name **irrational escalation of commitment**. It is seen in the famous bidding wars where titans of industry pay far more for acquisitions than they are worth. It can be seen on a small scale in an experiment called the **dollar auction**.

Originally invented by game theory people at Rand and Princeton, the dollar auction involves holding up a $5 bill and auctioning it off to the highest bidder. I do the exercise with my law students and MBA students. Negotiation trainers who appear before more affluent audiences have been known to use larger denominations. Bidding starts at 25 cents and moves in 25 cent increments. The high bidder gets the $5 bill. The difference between this auction and a regular auction is that the second-highest bidder has to pay the amount of his bid and gets nothing.

There is usually considerable interest at bids under a dollar. By the time we reach $2.50 (above which point I show a profit) there are only a few bidders left. At $5 there are only two. Bidders experience a certain psychological resistance at $5.00, but they are compelled forward by the same logic that drove earlier bids. "I can bid $5.25, get the five-dollar bill, and lose only 25 cents, or I can drop out now and pay $4.75 for nothing." The bidder facing the same problem at $5.50 makes the same determination. The bidding continues northward for what some observers find an extraordinarily long time and ends, typically, when one of the bidders simply does not have enough money to continue.

What is going on here? At the beginning there is the optimism that goes with the perceived opportunity to get something for nothing. As that perception fades, it is replaced by the desire to avoid loss. When it becomes obvious that some loss is inevitable, the goal becomes keeping losses minimized. And as that goal fades it is replaced by the desire to salvage self-respect by winning at any cost. In the final stage the "winner" is able to say, "I may have paid $17.50 for a $5 bill, but at least I got the $5 bill."

There are three lessons students are supposed to derive from this exercise. One is that it is important to prepare for a negotiation by thinking it through — and to think it through using the assumption that your opponent is just as clever and just as motivated as you are. The second is to avoid the sunk cost fallacy, the mistaken belief that you can somehow redeem earlier losses by throwing good money after bad. And the third is that it is important not to get distracted by ego and diverted by the emotions of battle — and forget what you came for.

§3.03(r) Biased Punctuation Of Conflict

Another way we persuade ourselves we are right is called **biased punctuation of conflict**. The Israelis and the Palestinians are a good example. When the I's blow up something belonging to the P's, they always justify it as retaliation for some earlier occasion when the P's blew up something that belonged to the I's. The P's don't see it that way. They see the previous explosion as retaliation for something the I's did before that. Each side punctuates the ongoing narrative so that each of its own strikes is justified and each of the other side's strikes is a fresh provocation. The mutual slaughter continues because each side punctuates the narrative in a way that makes their next move mandatory.

This results from a feature of human experience we discussed in §2.01(i), the fact that my experience is available to me and your experience is not. One consequence of this was shown in an experiment at the University of Texas. Subjects were asked to play the role of world leaders contemplating a nuclear strike. They made statements to one another followed by replies, followed by responses to those replies and so on. Some time later the subjects were shown some of the statements and asked what had been said just before or just after each statement was made. The finding was that the subjects could remember what they themselves did in response to statements by their opponents, but not what their opponents did in response to theirs. As the Harvard psychologist Daniel Gilbert put it in a July 24, 2007 *New York Times* op-ed, "[V]olunteers remembered the causes of their own statements and the consequences of their partner's."

Another result of this feature of our mental makeup is, again quoting Gilbert, "[T]he pain we receive seems more painful than the pain we produce." This was shown in an experiment at University College London. Subjects were assigned to pairs and connected to a device that measured precisely how much pressure each participant exerted onto the other's fingers. The subjects were told they were to apply exactly as much pressure to their partner's fingers as the partner had applied to theirs. The machine measured what really happened. And what really happened was that the experiment quickly degenerated into unpleasantness. According to the carefully calibrated measuring device, subjects trying their best to exert exactly as much pressure as had been exerted on them actually responded with about 40 percent more force than they had experienced.

What happens to me is different than what happens to you. Even when it's the same.

§3.03(s) Conversational Style

The failure of many negotiations has a similar cause. Because we tend to think of ourselves as occupying the Golden Mean, we tend to believe that when others say something, they mean what we would mean if we said that. This is the subject of the linguist Deborah Tannen's recorded lecture series *That's Not What I Meant! The sociolinguistics of everyday conversation* (Tannen, 2004, based on her 1986 book by that name). Some of us talk faster or louder than others; some of us stand closer or make more eye contact than others. Some of us use indirectness, others not. Some of us make listener noises to show we're paying attention; others not so much. These things vary by race, class, region, nationality, ethnicity, gender, age, even by profession.

The mistake is to think that these differences in what Tanner calls **conversational style** are really differences in ability or intention. People who talk quickly and use only brief pauses in conversational turn taking (think Northerners) are thought to be rude and pushy by their slower-talking Southern brethren. Correspondingly, Northerners tend to think their slower-talking Southern neighbors are dim-witted. Tannen says this pattern is repeated around the world. Swedes think Finns are stupid and Germans think Belgians are stupid for just the same reason.

To each of us, our own conversational style is invisible. It has no meaning; it is the box the meaning comes in. This is true when conversational styles match, but it is not true when they don't. "It's just not true that what you mean is what I would mean if I said what you said."

I have said many times in this book that awareness is key. The psychological tendency to see ourselves as occupying the Golden Mean at the center of the universe is gratifying, but it is not particularly helpful. The trick is to be aware of the tendency and to make allowance for it.

§3.03(t) Mental Accounting

We agreed earlier, I hope, that money is fungible — all dollars are the same as all other dollars — but that people do not behave as if they really believe it. When our perception of value is distorted by framing effects or regret aversion or the status quo bias, we treat some dollars as big, fat, important dollars and other dollars as almost weightless. We do it as well when our perception is distorted by the contrast effect or by the pull of a prominent solution. And it is the same error we commit when we allow ourselves to be influenced by the endowment effect, by anchoring, or by reactive devaluation.

A related problem comes about when we put certain dollars into special categories and resist moving them even when it makes clear economic sense. Here is an example adapted from work by Richard Thaler (Belsky & Gilovich, 1999, p. 33).

Suppose you had two $50 tickets to a show and two $50 bills to spend on a fancy dinner. You get to the restaurant and discover you lost the bills. The maitre d' offers to buy your tickets for $100. Do you sell the tickets, skip the show, and have dinner? Or do you skip dinner, keep the tickets and see the show?

New case, same setup. You get to the restaurant and discover you lost the tickets. The maitre d' offers to sell you two tickets for $100. Do you buy the tickets, skip dinner, and see the show. Or do you skip the show and have dinner?

Once again, the answer we might predict is that people who especially like fancy dinners will choose to eat dinner in both cases and people who especially like shows will choose the show in both cases. And, once again, that isn't the result we find when we do the experiment. People who lost the tickets tend to eat. People who lost the money tend to choose to see the show. Why should this be?

I suspect part of the answer lies in our belief in a just world and the belief that things happen for a reason. "Our steps are guided," as a colleague of mine says. If I lost the tickets, the thinking goes, it must be because The Divine Plan for My Life doesn't include my seeing the show.

But there is another explanation for this preference reversal. The literature calls it mental accounting, and it works like this. I paid $100 for those tickets that I lost. If I spend another $100 on new tickets, I will have spent $200 on this show. The show might be worth $100, but it isn't worth $200. Eat dinner.

If I lost the money, the thinking is the same. I figure that $100 was money I was going to spend on dinner. If I sell the tickets and spend the proceeds on dinner I will effectively have spent $200 on dinner. That's too much to spend on dinner. See the show.

You can see that this comes about because I have set up different accounts in my head — hence "mental accounting." But the whole idea of money is that it is legal tender for all debts public and private. It doesn't have designated categories, types and sub-types. None of it is sacred. If you are keeping money in a bank savings account earning 2 percent and at the same time you are carrying a credit card balance and paying 28 percent, you are not being prudent and careful and responsibly guarding your savings. You are being stupid.

All money is the same. There is no such thing as special money, and there is no such thing as free money or the house's money. Few of us really believe this, and even fewer consistently act as if they believe it, but it is certainly true.

The effective negotiator uses this feature of the psychological landscape to his advantage. If you can convince your negotiation opponent that certain of your funds are sacred, you can often get him to stop asking for them. If you can convince him that certain of his funds are the house's money, you can get him to give them up without as much of a fight. It is a matter of packaging.

For example, take the premium you pay at the gas station for the privilege of paying with a credit card. The gas station doesn't want to tell you that you are paying a premium; people don't like paying premiums. So instead it tells you there is a discount for paying with cash. We don't so much mind not getting a discount. Of course, getting a discount for paying cash is exactly equivalent to paying a premium for using a credit card. Exactly. But one is acceptable and one is not, because of the way the information is processed.

In California the legislature has written this foolishness into law. According to the California Civil Code:

> §1748.1(a) No retailer in any sales, service, or lease transaction with a consumer may impose a surcharge on a cardholder who elects to use a credit card in lieu of payment by cash, check, or similar means. A retailer may, however, offer discounts for the purpose of inducing payment by cash, check, or other means not involving the use of a credit card, provided that the discount is offered to all prospective buyers.

A similar manipulation of packaging was proposed by Republican consultant Frank Luntz when he advised 2006 congressional candidates:

> You may be tempted to talk about making the tax cuts from 2001 and 2003 "permanent." Don't. It's far more effective to talk about "the largest tax hike in American history if these tax cuts are revoked." Remember, the American public dislikes a tax hike more than they like a tax cut. (Shleifer, 2006)

§3.03(u) Timing Effects

The pattern is clear. Thinking about our decisions is expensive and difficult. When we can, we avoid it in favor of easy-to-remember heuristics. The word "free" is powerful for this reason. If something is free, we don't have to think about it any more. If it's free, we'll take it. If it is not free, we have to consider the question.

The same thing is true of "now." We have a strong bias in favor of now. Put another way, we apply a discount to things that will happen in the future. This is consistent with our evolutionary psychology perspective. In the ancestral environment the future was a very iffy proposition. Life expectancy beyond the next few hours was a great deal more chancy than it is today. There was no saving for retirement because there was neither saving nor retirement. This habit of thinking appears to have come down to us in the form of the future discount.

Behavioral economist David Laibson explains **timing effects** nicely:

> People very robustly want instant gratification right now, and want to be patient in the future. If you ask people, "Which do you want right now, fruit or chocolate?" they say, "Chocolate!" But if you ask, "Which one a week from now?" they will say, "Fruit." *Now* we want chocolate, cigarettes, and a trashy movie. In the *future* we want to eat fruit, to quit smoking, and to watch Bergman films." (Quoted in Lambert, 2006. Italics in original.)

This explains why it always seems like a good idea to start that diet and exercise program tomorrow. If I start it today, I pay for it in today's full units of value but get rewarded in heavily discounted future units. If I start tomorrow, the payment and the reward are both discounted.

The classical economist's approach to the question of whether I should contribute to my IRA or not, or eat a salad rather than a cheeseburger, assumes that I will add up all the benefit I will gain over the rest of my life from either choice and choose the outcome with the highest total value. Since, to a rational actor, a unit of suffering is the same whether it endured now or later, the IRA and the salad should win every time. But that ain't how it works.

Richard Thaler tells about a dermatologist who can't get her patients to avoid the sun by warning them about skin cancer. She gets much more compliance when she tells them "it can cause large pores and blackheads" (Thaler, 1992, p. 94).

Here is a different timing effect. Suppose I have seven presents for you. Do you want them all at once or spaced out over a week? Now suppose I have to pull out seven of your teeth. Same question, do you want them all out at once or one a day for a week? The tendency, I think you will agree, is to segregate gains and integrate losses. This has to do with the principle of diminishing marginal utility. The classic example of that concept is the familiar experience that the first piece of pizza is more delicious than the fourth.

So, another packaging feature EN is careful to take into account when structuring proposals is the relationship of the payoff to the present. We discount the future both in terms of payoff and sacrifice. We prefer to segregate gains and integrate losses. And the principle of diminishing marginal utility is at work in our valuation of payoffs.

The careful reader will have noticed that there is a tension, if not a contradiction, between some of these effects and others. The careful reader will be correct. I have only the most mealymouthed of replies. People are complicated, and the systematic study of these matters is very new.

This is good and bad. The bad news is that our understanding is spotty and messy. The good news is that there is an opportunity here for some clever person to take up the issue and figure it out. As I see it, the area of decision theory in general and its application to dispute resolution in particular is something like 19th century physical science. There are still plenty of discoveries to be made by the equivalent of amateur tinkerers in basement laboratories and garage workshops. I offer a few of my own suggestions in Chapter 5.

§3.03(v) Position Effects

Psychologists Richard Nisbett and Timothy Wilson put four pairs of nylon panty hose on a table at a big-box discount store not far from where I live, and encouraged people to examine them and rate their quality. The nylons were arranged from left to right and labeled A, B, C and D. Almost all the subjects expressed a preference.

Twelve percent preferred pair A, 17 percent preferred pair B, 31 percent pair C, and 40 percent pair D. The subjects gave lots of reasons for their preferences: sheerness, elasticity, weave, and so on. None said they chose the pair they did because of its position in the display. When Nisbett and Wilson asked directly if position had anything to do with their choice, all except one psychology student "looked at us suspiciously and said of course not" (Wilson, 2002, p. 103).

At this point in this book, you are probably not surprised to learn that all the nylons were identical and that there is a name for this. It is called a **position effect**.

As mentioned in §3.01(a), juries reach different verdicts depending on whether the harsher or the more lenient verdict is presented for discussion first. This is called an **order effect**. We also sometimes display an effect known as **extremeness aversion**. Given a choice of several objects, we tend to avoid the ones at either end. Our preference is for the compromise choice in the middle, as we saw in our discussion of bread machines in §3.03(d).

None of us believe we are subject to these effects, but the evidence is that we are. Again, the precise boundaries of the effects and the results of the complex interactions of multiple effects are not well understood — at least not by me. The best I can do is to point out that they exist and that, for defensive purposes if nothing else, we ought to be aware of them. If your negotiation opponent offers you a choice of several options, ask yourself if you would make the same choice if the same options had been presented differently.

§3.03(w) Certainty Effect

System 1 works in very simple terms. "Me food now," it says, and it motivates our actions. It has a problem with delayed gratification, as we've seen. It wants what it wants when it wants it. And it's not very smart. Not having done its math homework during the Pleistocene, it never mastered even the fundamental concepts of probability. So it makes numerical decisions on an impressionistic basis. "Free" is good. Loss is bad.

System 1 likes certainty; it's a concept it can deal with. Probability is too complicated. We favor outcomes that are certain over those that are merely probable. Fair enough. But "the reduction in probability from certainty (1) to a degree of uncertainty (.8) produces a more pronounced loss in attractiveness than a corresponding reduction from one level of uncertainty (.25) to another (.2)" (Thompson, 1998, p. 89). In other words, "People tend to simplify their thinking about probability into categories of sure thing (certain), possible, or impossible" (Baron, 2000, p. 258). A probability of 1.0 is something we can understand. An event with a probability of 1.0 is going to happen. An event with a probability of .998, on the other hand, is iffy. We will pay far more to get that last .002 that takes us to 1.0 than we will pay to get from .996 to .998. We overweight certainty.

The same is true at the other end of the probability scale. This is a confound called the **possibility effect**. We overweight the difference between a probability of .002 and a probability of zero. An event with a probability of .002, or .00002, is possible. An event with a probability of zero is not. We are far more willing than is rational to bet on events with vanishingly low probability.

The possibility effect also gives us a familiar line of cross-examination questions. I remember watching a defense lawyer examine a police witness about a trail of blood that led from a dead body to his client. It came out that the police lab had not tested each sample of blood in the trail. That was counsel's opening. "It's possible, isn't it, that each sample came from a different person?" Right. Some unknown number of bleeding people may have walked by and dropped blood samples on the ground in just such a way that it appeared to be a trail leading to your client. That's possible.

Bad lawyers make that silly mistake all the time. But they wouldn't do it if it didn't have some resonance. People are bad at evaluating or comparing probabilities, and we avoid doing it when we can. The simplest way to avoid calculating probabilities is to divide outcomes into those that are sure things and those that are not.

The classic experiments that show the certainty effect, and something called the **pseudocertainty effect**, involve viruses and vaccines (Piatelli-Palmarini, 1994, p. 85; Plous, 1993, p. 101). We very predictably make demonstrably bad choices when confronted with risk and the ability to avoid risk. Piatelli-Palmarini found his subjects were willing to pay:

- $800 to eliminate a 1-in-1,000 risk of serious illness; or
- $250 to reduce the risk from 4 in 1,000 to 3 in 1,000

but would require a payment of:

- $100,000 before they would voluntarily accept a risk of 1 in 1,000.

As we have said many times, whatever the value is that you ascribe to something, that value shouldn't change depending on the package. A 1-in-1,000 risk of death is a 1-in-1,000 risk of death. If you could buy it or sell it, it ought to have a relatively stable price. But that isn't the way we work.

The pseudocertainty effect accounts for an experiment conducted by Slovic, Fischhoff and Lichtenstein. In it, there was one vaccine that was expected to work half the time, and another that worked all the time but only on one of two diseases that a subject was equally likely to contract. In other words, the vaccines were exactly equivalent. But more people were willing to take the second one than the first. Why should this be?

"The vaccine was more popular in the pseudocertainty condition because it appeared to eliminate risk rather than simply reduce it" (Plous, 1993, p. 101).

Plous goes on to explain that marketers are aware of the pseudocertainty effect. This accounts for the prevalence of gimmicks like "Clean three shirts and the fourth one is free." That formulation is perceived as better than a plain 25 percent price reduction (to which it is, of course, equivalent).

The elimination of risk is, obviously, one of the principle reasons litigants choose to settle lawsuits rather than try them. The effective negotiator is aware of the power of this principle.

§3.03(x) Priming And Schemas

Experimenters put a group of subjects to work on the task of unscrambling anagrams. Half the group is randomly assigned to unscramble words having to do with the elderly — words like "wise," "bingo," and "Florida." The other half unscrambles neutral words like "thirsty," "clean," and "private." When they finish, the experimenters thank them for their time and say goodbye. Then, unknown to the subjects, the experimenters time how long it takes them to walk to the elevator. The subjects "primed" with the elderly "schema" take an appreciably longer time to shuffle down the hall.

Leigh Thompson defines **schemas** as "cognitive structures which consist of our knowledge, beliefs, and expectations pertaining to some stimulus domain, containing both factual, objective information and subjective impressions" (1998, p. 308). She defines **priming** as "an enhancement of the processing of a stimulus as a function of prior exposure" (p. 304).

Cordelia Fine has an easier way to think of it. She says groups of brain cells sleep in big schema beds together. When we shake some cells awake, we also rouse the others who sleep in the same bed and make them more likely to wake up. Whether or not this is the case in terms of neuroanatomy, it certainly appears to be the case experimentally. We seem to have a large number of these schemas in our heads, and when they are primed we behave in certain, predictable ways.

Using another word-scramble task, researchers found that people who received a "rude" prime (e.g., through words such as "disturb," "intrude," "brazen") were quicker to interrupt an experimenter. Other research finds that covert primes for helpfulness make people more helpful, and intelligence primes (words that activate a stereotype of a college professor) make people perform better at Trivial Pursuit (Zaltman, 2003, p. 116).

Another researcher concluded that the scent from a hidden bottle of household cleanser primed the cleanliness schema and made subjects more likely to clean up their cookie crumbs.

Recent research by scientists in Belgium examined what happens when the schema being primed has to do with sex. Male subjects were asked to play the ultimatum game (described in §1.01) after they had looked at pictures of landscapes in one experimental condition or pictures of young models in bikinis in the other. Other subjects were tested after being asked to handle either a t-shirt or a bra. The idea was to measure whether the men behaved differently in the economic game depending on whether they had been exposed to a sex cue or not.

The answer is that they did. Many men will accept a less favorable split in the ultimatum game after exposure to a sex cue than without one. A proposed explanation for the finding is this. The limbic system of the male brain (System 1), exposed to visual images of sexy women or pieces of women's underwear, believes it is in proximity to a mating opportunity. When there is a mating opportunity in the neighborhood, the male is going to increase his chances of success if he can. Having something of value with which to impress the potential mate is likely to help. Now is not the time to worry about getting the best possible deal or to stand on principle or to build one's reputation as a tough bargainer. Now is the time to ensure you have something rather than nothing. The brain says "Take the money! We need some bling!" (Hopkin, 2006).

Further out on the strangeness scale, a study by Geoffrey Miller at the University of New Mexico recently published in *Evolution and Human Behavior* clocked the per shift earnings of lap dancers at "gentlemen's clubs" and mapped them against their menstrual cycles. Women who were ovulating made an average of $335 per shift. Women in the infertile part of their cycle, or who were taking birth control pills and thus had their fertility suppressed, earned an average of $185. The precise working of the estrus cue in this experiment is covert, but it appears to be priming the mating schema and getting these men up off of their wallets (Miller, Tybur & Jordan, 2007).

I will leave it to the reader to determine how best to incorporate these insights into his or her professional practice.

A fascinating body of work has been produced by the social psychologists Sheldon Solomon, Jeff Greenberg and Tom Pyszczynski on the subject of death cues. In study after study, subjects whose death schemas have been primed demonstrate a particular type of response. They cling to the symbols of their worldviews. Since the world view of a trial court judge, for instance, is tied to a strong belief in obedience to the law, the scientists predicted that municipal judges who had been reminded of their mortality would be inclined to punish lawbreakers more harshly than judges who were not. They arranged to have a group of 22 judges set bail in the case of an imaginary prostitute. The files for the accused were identical. But in the experimental condition the judges were first asked to provide written responses to two questions about their own death.

Result? The judges who were just asked to review the file and determine the bond set it at an average of $50. The judges whose death schemas had been primed set it at an average of $455 (Pyszczynski, Solomon & Greenberg, p. 46).

For our purposes as mediators and negotiators the work on priming and schemas has two important consequences. The downside implication is the scary notion that these schemas are in our heads, that they can be primed, and that marketers and other evil-doers are figuring out how to prime them. (The preceding Zaltman quotation comes from a book called *How Customers Think*. Gerald Zaltman is a Professor of Marketing at the Harvard Business School and a Fellow at Harvard University's interdisciplinary Mind/Brain/Behavior Initiative.) The principle of the co-evolution of predator and prey that I mentioned in §3.03(e) and will mention again in Chapter 6 requires that those of us who are the food source for Professor Zaltman's marketing practitioners must ourselves become more aware of these subjects. The alternative is too horrible to contemplate.

The other implication is far more sanguine. According to Pyszczynski, Solomon and Greenberg, the opposite of mortality salience is self-esteem. When subjects are given cues that prime the self-esteem schema they react more openly, more freely, less fearfully. If I'm not mistaken, this is what **transformative mediation** is about.

Defining empowerment and recognition in *The Promise of Mediation*, Bush and Folger say this:

> In the most general terms, empowerment is achieved when disputing parties experience a strengthened awareness of their own self-worth and their own ability to deal with whatever difficulties they face, regardless of external constraints. Recognition is achieved when, given some degree of empowerment, disputing parties experience an expanded willingness to acknowledge and be responsive

> to other parties' situations and common human qualities. (Bush & Folger, 1994, p. 84)

Notwithstanding the difference in terminology, what Pyszczynski et al. have done is provide scientific verification of the central Bush and Folger intuition.

§3.04 WHY MEDIATION WORKS

In his widely cited book *Influence: The psychology of persuasion*, Cialdini (1993) says that the many ways salespeople, politicians, con artists, and other influence professionals get us to do their bidding all boil down to one or another of these six "weapons of influence": authority, liking, commitment-consistency, reciprocity, social proof, and scarcity. We have touched upon each of them in previous sections. Mediation works because it uses all six. Let's see how.

Even before the litigant walks into the mediator's office, he is prepared to be impressed with the mediator's authority. The expectation is that the mediator will have the knowledge, experience, and ability to get the parties out of an intractable dispute — that he knows magic techniques and mysteries, like a medical specialist or witch doctor. When the litigant does walk into the office, he meets someone with the badges and indicia of authority. A secretary greets visitors, takes coats, offers coffee. The litigant waits, just enough to demonstrate that the mediator is busy with important matters. The mediator then emerges — sporting a dark suit, white shirt, silk tie, shiny black shoes, and gray temples, or feminine equivalents — and takes the litigant to a room with leather chairs, long table, thick books, and dark paneling. This is the authority weapon at work.

The mediator, powerful and busy as he is, shakes hands and smiles warmly. He makes sure the litigant has fresh coffee. He makes friendly small talk about the weather or the traffic or the parking. Did you give your parking ticket to the secretary to have it validated? No? He takes your ticket and summons the secretary.

He could sit behind the big desk, but he doesn't. He sits directly across from the litigant with nothing between them. Both feet on the floor, he looks the litigant in the eye, leans forward and asks "How can I help?" He listens actively. He paraphrases and validates.

He mirrors. Rich and powerful as he obviously is, he understands and he wants to help. He cares. This is the liking weapon.

Then he gets the commitment he's been setting up during all that listening. He asks, "It sounds to me like you are tired of this litigation and you would like to get past it and get on with your life. Is that right?" Or, "It sounds to me like you are concerned this litigation is having a negative effect on little Wanda June. Is that right? And you would like to get it settled so your lives can return to normal?" We're not here to punish your opponent for being a crook or to teach your rotten ex-spouse a lesson, right? We're here because you want to get this matter behind you and get back to what's really important. Is that what I hear you saying? That's the commitment and consistency weapon.

Then the negotiation enters the explicit bargaining phase. There are offers and counter-offers, back and forth. The reciprocity norm is the weapon used to extract them. He moved last, now it's your turn. You want the other side to make a concession, you make one.

So far the mediator has not said anything evaluative. He has been functioning mainly as a facilitator, helping you frame issues, helping you express interests, helping you look for outcomes that maximize mutual gains. But there comes a time when the mediator will be asked to give some evaluative advice. What do you think, Mr. Mediator? You have seen a lot of these cases. You know the judges in this jurisdiction. You're familiar with the jury awards. You know these lawyers. Is this a good deal or not?

There are mediation purists who will tell you a mediator should not answer that question. I am not one of them. I think a fair assessment of the market value of your case is one of the reasons to go to a mediator. I think a mediator has a duty to tell a party who asks. "In my experience, cases like yours in this jurisdiction tend to settle in the range of $x to $y. That's not to say you won't get more; maybe you will. That's not to say you should settle for $x. It's your decision, and you should do what you think is best. But you should make that decision based on the best information you can get." This is the social proof weapon. Most people in your situation do S. If you do S, you won't be out there all alone.

Finally, the settlement offer on the table will be available for a limited time only. If your opponent has to go back and conduct more depositions and retain an expert and all the rest, his costs will go up and his settlement demand will go up. Right now we've got a proposed deal on the table and everyone has done the work necessary to get us there. We can agree and walk out of here with the deal closed and the case behind us. Or we can reject. It's up to you. But if we don't reach agreement now, it is very likely the deal will unravel, the good-will will go away, and we will start back at the beginning. Or worse. This is the scarcity weapon.

Put them all together, and it's no wonder mediation is such an effective form of dispute resolution.

4

Agreements

Leigh Thompson, in her book *The Heart and Mind of the Negotiator*, outlines a three-tiered pyramid model of successful agreements. Level One agreements, she says, are those where each party judges his outcome to be better than he could have achieved away from the table. In other words, each party has achieved a deal that is better than his BATNA. Since it is irrational for a negotiator to enter an agreement where the payoff is not as good as some available alternative, we expect all agreements to be Level One agreements. If they are not, if a party has a better alternative away from the table, we would expect him to decline.

To use language from an earlier part of our discussion, if the offer on the table does not exceed the negotiator's reservation point, the proposed deal is not within the Zone of Possible Agreement (the ZOPA) and the negotiator will not agree to it. Accordingly, all deals that settle are Level One deals.

A Level Two agreement is not just better than the non-agreement alternatives; it is also better than other possible agreements. Let's go back to the example about dividing fruit. There are six apples and six oranges. If we can agree on a division, we get to keep the fruit. If we can't, we have to go to court where the process will take six years, the lawyers will take all our money, and the fruit will have long rotted away by the time a resolution is reached. In this situation any agreement we reach to divide the fruit among us will be better than our non-agreement alternative.

Let's suppose you value oranges at 3 units of value each, and apples at only 2 units. And let's suppose I have the complementary preference: I value oranges at 2 units and apples at 3.

The Level One agreement that gives us each three oranges and three apples nets you 15 units of value (3 X 3 = 9 for the oranges, plus 3 X 2 = 6 for the apples) and nets me 15 units of value (3 X 2 = 6 for the oranges, plus 3 X 3 = 9 for the apples). That's the obvious, prominent, compromise solution.

A Level Two agreement is one that improves on that outcome. If we agree you get 4 oranges and 2 apples, you net 16 units of value instead of 15. Giving me an extra apple increases my net value too. I get 16 units out of this deal as well. This is what it means to improve mutual gains. The total amount of happiness units generated by the prominent solution was 30, 15 for you and 15 for me. Tweaking the solution in the way we just did generates 16 units for you and 16 for me for a total of 32.

Note that we accomplished this without adding any fruit to the system. And we did it without adding any altruism. We improved the payoffs for both parties by learning more about their preferences and matching preferences to outcomes. And we can do it again.

I look at the new deal and see you still have 2 apples and I still have 2 oranges. Since you were willing to trade an apple for an orange before, I ask you if you would be willing to do it again. You would. The result is 17 units of happiness for each of us for a total of 34.

Same thing. No additional fruit, no altruism. I am not interested in your outcome because I care about your happiness. I'm interested in your outcome because I care about *my* happiness. But I can't make a deal by myself. I need you to agree. And you will only agree to a deal that increases your happiness (or, at least, leaves you no worse off).

You still have one apple and I still have one orange. Want to trade? You do. Now you have 6 oranges for a total of 18 happiness units; I have 6 apples for a total of 18; and there is a grand total of 36 units of happiness realized in the deal.

At this point, there is no amount of further shuffling that would make one party better off without making the other party worse off. We have arrived at Level Three. The formal name for the condition we have reached is **Pareto-optimal**, named after the mathematician Vilfredo Pareto, who invented it. A solution is Pareto-optimal if no other distribution of value could make one party better off without making another party worse off.

It is a worthy goal for negotiators to attempt to reach Pareto-optimal results. It is not the only goal, however. Pareto-optimality is a measure of efficiency. A solution is efficient if it accounts for all the value in the system. It is inefficient if the parties leave value on the table, if they walk away while there are still opportunities to improve mutual gain. But please note two things about Pareto-optimal results. First, there is not just one Pareto-optimal solution, there are many. They are said to lie along a curve called the **Pareto-optimal frontier** (Figure 3).

The second is that any solution that lies along the Pareto-optimal frontier — any solution that distributes all the value available in the system — is a Pareto-optimal result, no matter how one-sided. It would be Pareto-optimal in our example, for instance, if I got all the apples *and* all the oranges. From that point there could be no further redistribution of fruits that would improve your outcome without making mine worse.

About The Pareto-Optimal Frontier

Figure 3 on page 148 is another view of the ZOPA and also shows the Pareto-optimal frontier, the ZOPA's outer boundary. The table below describes additional relationships within the frontier diagram.

Vertical axis	Represents Party 1's outcome. Party 1 prefers outcomes the further up they appear.
Horizontal axis	Represents Party 2's outcome. Party 2 prefers outcomes the further to the right they appear.
Parallel line above horizontal axis	Party 1 will not accept any outcome below that line, which crosses the vertical axis at Party 1's reservation point.
Parallel line to right of vertical axis	Party 2 will not accept any outcome to the left of that line, which crosses the horizontal axis at Party 2's reservation point.
Shaded area (ZOPA)	Represents all possible deals — the Zone of Possible Agreement.
Curved boundary of of ZOPA area	Deals on the outer boundary of the ZOPA are called Pareto-optimal because they fully distribute the resources being negotiated. The curved boundary line as a whole is called the Pareto-optimal frontier.

A ➪ B

From any proposed settlement point inside the ZOPA and not on the Pareto frontier, it is possible to improve the outcome for one party without reducing the outcome for the other, by moving toward the frontier along a line parallel to the benefiting party's axis. For example, moving from a proposed settlement at point A to point B improves Party 1's outcome without reducing Party 2's outcome.

C ➪ D

Similarly, moving from Point C to point D improves the settlement outcome for Party 2 without reducing the outcome for Party 1.

Point E

Outside of the ZOPA, deals are impossible because there simply isn't enough stuff in the deal. If Party 1 and Party 2 are dividing 4 oranges, Point E might represent a proposed deal in which "each party gets 3."

G ➪ F

or

F ➪ G

Once a deal is Pareto-optimal, it is not possible to improve the outcome for one party without reducing the outcome for the other party. Note that any movement to the right along the frontier (an improvement for Party 2) is also movement down (a reduction for Party 1); conversely, any movement up along the frontier (an improvement for Party 1) is also a movement to the left (a reduction for Party 2).

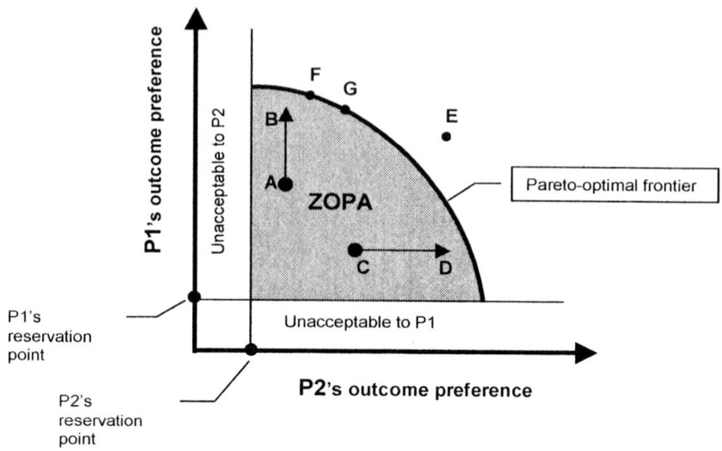

Figure 3. Pareto-Optimal Frontier

§4.01 COUNTERFACTUALS

Fester and Karbunkle share a cab to the airport. Both of them have 5:00 PM flights. The cab gets stuck in traffic, and they don't get to the airport until 6:30, an hour-and-a-half late. Fester's flight left on time, but Karbunkle's left an hour-and-15-minutes late. Both men missed their flights, but who feels worse? (Piatelli-Palmarini, 1994, p. 28)

I think we all instinctively agree that Karbunkle, who just missed his flight by a few minutes, feels worse than Fester, who missed his by an hour and a half, but why? I won't indulge here in speculation in terms of evolutionary psychology or neurophysiology, tempting as such speculation may be. I'll just note for the record that a careful negotiator would be well advised to pay attention to this kind of observation. If I want my negotiation opponent to feel bad, I might look for a way to present a missed opportunity as just barely missed. If I want him not to feel so bad, I might present the missed opportunity as long missed.

Try another thought experiment: Two people, creatively called A and B, are standing in separate lines. A is in line at a greasy cheeseburger joint when a smiley man comes up and says, "Congratulations, you are our 1,000th customer; here's a check for $100." B is standing in line at a different greasy place when a man comes up to *the guy in front of B* and says, "Congratulations, you are our 10,000th customer; here is a check for $1,000. Then he turns to B and says, "And here's $150 for you."

Who would you rather be, A or B?

It turns out that many people would rather be A (Belsky and Gilovich, 1999, p. 98). They would rather be A and get $100 than be B and get $150, if being B means they have to watch the guy in front of them get $1,000. In other words, it matters how we frame the **counterfactuals**. Counterfactuals are what didn't happen; hypotheticals, what ifs. Although they are contrary to fact, they have an important influence on how we view what did happen.

As we've discussed, we don't judge our condition on an absolute scale; we judge it on a relative scale. Am I cold? Am I rich? Am I happy? I'm not as cold as I was a few minutes ago. I'm not as rich as Jones. I'm happier than Smith. That's the only way we can do it. A negotiator who can pick the measuring scale can control the opponent's feeling about the deal.

A $0.50 per hour raise can be presented to an $8.00-per-hour employee in several ways. You can call it a 6.25 percent raise. You can call it a raise of over a thousand dollars a year. You can say it's not as good as the $0.75 the guys in the plant across the street got. You can say it's a helluva lot better than the layoff notices the guys in the plant down the street got. He who picks the comparators rules the deal.

Here's a famous example of the same idea. Think of the medal stands at the Olympics: gold, silver, and bronze. Think about the person standing on that gold-medal stand. Happiest guy in the world, right? Right. No question there. Now think about those other two guys, the one who won the silver medal and the one who got the bronze. Who do you think is happier?

When pictures of medal winners were presented to experimental subjects who had no idea which athlete had won which medal, they consistently rated the bronze-medal winners as happier looking than the silver-medal winners. Why? (Medvec, Madey & Gilovich, 1995)

It has to do with choosing the comparator. The guy standing on the silver-medal stand compares himself to the guy who won the gold. The counterfactual in his head goes, "If only I had run a thousandth of a second faster or jumped an inch higher, that could be me." The guy on the bronze-medal stand compares himself to all the rest of the world. He won a medal at the Olympics. Compared to everyone else in the world, he's doing great.

§4.02 THE PEAK-END RULE

One more. Take a population of 50-somethings on their way in to get their colonoscopy examinations. Half the group gets the colonoscopy the regular, thoroughly unpleasant way: The physician inserts the scope, wiggles it around for an impossibly long time and takes it out. The other half gets precisely the same examination for exactly the same length of time, but at the end of the procedure, instead of removing the scope, the physician leaves it in place for an additional 30 seconds without wiggling it around. When it's over, both groups are asked to rate the experience and to predict how likely they are to return to have it done again. What result?

The rational expectation would be that the second group had a worse experience than the first. After all, they experienced everything the first group did plus an additional 30 seconds of unpleasantness. But that is not what the patients reported. Subjects in the second group reported that they found the experience significantly less disagreeable than subjects in the first group, and they rated themselves more likely to return for follow ups. How can this be?

It turns out that we judge our experiences according to what researchers call a **peak-end rule**. We pay attention to how good or bad an experience is at its peak and at the end.

This accounts for the common negotiation advice that you should arrange to be the one to make the last concession. Even if dealing with you has been painful up to that point, if you agree to concede to your opponent on the final round, it will leave a good taste in his mouth. He will tend to evaluate the entire experience according to the peak-end rule and will be more likely to agree to deal with you again.

§4.03 POST-SETTLEMENT SETTLEMENT

How do we get from a Level One agreement, an agreement that is merely better than our BATNA, to a more Pareto-efficient agreement? In order to do this, the parties must "log-roll": trade off issues that are of more value to one in exchange for those that are of more value to the other. But several factors stand in the way of our being able to do that. One is fixed-pie perception — the belief that our opponents value the same things we do and that our interests are directly opposed. Another is our reluctance to disclose which issues are truly valuable to us because of our fear that our opponents will use such knowledge against us.

A third obstruction is the tangled web of exaggerations, distortions, and misleading statements we made earlier in the bargaining process to keep our opponent from learning our true interests. If I have been transferred out of town, and every week I fail to sell my house is a week in which I have to make two mortgage payments, I am going to carefully guard that information. The last thing I want a potential buyer to know is that I am desperate to sell. Similarly, if you have just been transferred into town and you're desperate to find a place before you have to move your family into a motel, you're not going to tell me about it.

Such a situation sets up a potential "Gift of the Magi" scenario — the O. Henry story where she sells her hair to buy him a watch fob for Christmas and he sells his watch to buy tortoise-shell combs for her hair. Perhaps my attempt to sell you my house is not quite as beautiful and tragic as the O. Henry story, but the loss of a potentially elegant deal because of our mutual distrust would certainly be sad.

There are a few things we can do to avoid this sadness. One of them we have already discussed. To the extent we are able to build trust in the early stages of negotiation, we decrease the likelihood of misrepresentation. If we have schmoozed successfully, there is a chance our opponent will voluntarily disclose his true interest.

If not, we have another chance during the bargaining phase. The EN asks hypothetical questions. "Suppose I was able to offer you the house sooner, would that be of interest to you?" He asks lots of open-ended questions throughout bargaining in order to tease out just this kind of information. The multiple offers we discussed in §3.03(e) are another attempt to achieve the same thing. An opponent who will not tell you he is pressed for time in so many words may nevertheless show a preference for an option that reduces time over one that reduces cost. EN is watching carefully for just that kind of intelligence.

If none of those techniques succeeds, there is still one more available. Called **post-settlement settlement**, it is the brainchild of Howard Raiffa, author of *The Art and Science of Negotiation* (1982), a classic work in the field.

The idea is this. We have reached a deal we are prepared to live with, a deal we know is at least better than our respective BATNAs. But before we ink it, we agree to engage in a process of hypothetical, suggested trade-offs. If any of the suggested trade-offs is better for both of us (ideally), or at least better for one of us without harming the other, then we adopt it.

Another way to put it is this: When we were negotiating the deal, each of us had a BATNA away from the table. We have reached a point where the deal on the table is better for each of us than our respective BATNAs. We have a Level One deal. We are attempting to tweak the deal to get it to Level Two. But now that we have a Level One deal in hand, our best alternative to an improved deal is not our original BATNAs, it is the Level One deal on the table.

You may have been withholding the information that you need to sell quickly. I may have been withholding the information that I need to move quickly. That made perfect sense when we feared that information could be exploited by our opponents. But now we have a deal that is better than our available alternatives. Disclosure at this point can only improve our outcome; it can't hurt. So it no longer makes sense for us to withhold or misrepresent.

Confident that we have achieved a Level One deal, we can work together to try to get it to Level Two or Three. We have nothing to lose.

It is not clear that post-settlement settlement works. Some studies have supported the idea (Thompson, 1998, p. 60). Others have not (Shell, 1999, p. 191). For our purposes, perhaps it is sufficient to know that the concept of post-settlement settlement exists, that the idea of increased Pareto-efficiency exists, and that one may lead to the other. Armed with these concepts, we may be able to enrich our practice with some variation of post-settlement settlement to achieve some species of improved Pareto-efficiency without introducing a new full-blown, formal process.

§4.04 GLOATING

This is related to another old salesman's gimmick — the plea for mercy. "Boy, you sure drive a hard bargain. You're cleaning me out." An effective negotiator convinces his opponent that the opponent got a good deal.

Meltsner and Schrag say this: "*Make your adversary feel good.* Never gloat over the terms of a settlement. Not only is such behavior boorish, but it may provoke an adversary to reopen negotiations or to adopt a different and stronger negotiating posture the next time you deal with him...." (Goldberg, Sander & Rogers, 1992, p. 22)

And the Proverbs of Solomon says this: It is naught, it is naught, saith the buyer: but when he is gone his way, then he boasteth. (Proverbs 20:14)

The moral for our purposes is that the effective negotiator boasteth not until he has gone his way.

§4.05 A WARNING

Nobel Prize winner Daniel Kahneman and his colleague Jonathan Renshon reviewed the biases, heuristics, and cognitive illusions discovered in the last 40 years of psychological research. They were looking to see whether the biases tended to favor hawks or doves, cooperators or defectors.

> [W]e were startled by what we found: All of the biases in our list favor hawks. These psychological impulses ... incline national leaders to exaggerate the evil intentions of adversaries, to misjudge how adversaries perceive them, to be overly sanguine when hostilities start, and overly

> reluctant to make necessary concessions in negotiations. In short, these biases have the effect of making wars more likely to begin, and more difficult to end. (Kahneman & Renshon, 2007)

This was written for an article in *Foreign Policy*, so the emphasis is on international relations and the actions of heads of state. But the lesson is clear for those of us working at a more retail level. For reasons we can only speculate about, evolution has provided us with a set of psychological features that incline us toward the aggressive stance in negotiation and litigation.

Loss aversion, self-serving bias, the fundamental attribution error, overconfidence, biased punctuation of conflict, and the others tend to make compromise more distasteful and settlement more difficult. To an unfortunate extent, our efforts at conciliation and dispute resolution are working against type, against our information processing strategies and our natural psychological disposition.

Hawks are sometimes right, Kahneman and Renshon acknowledge at the end of their article. But "understanding the biases that most of us harbor can at least help ensure that the hawks don't win more arguments than they should."

5

Experiments

Once a basic understanding of cognitive heuristics is in place, the next question, of course, is How can we use this understanding to improve our effectiveness as negotiators and mediators? The model for my answer to this question comes from a clever little gimmick called **prospective hindsight**.

Experimentalists like Baruch Fischhoff have demonstrated what they call **hindsight bias**. This is the familiar impulse to believe "I knew it all along." Things that were not at all clear when they were still in the future appear to have been inevitable once they are safely in the past. It's what makes Monday morning quarterbacking so much easier than the real-time kind.

The beauty of prospective hindsight is that it uses this feature of our cognitive apparatus in a way that improves our thinking rather than distorting it. To use it, we try to imagine looking *back* at a decision that lies in the future and use the hindsight bias in advance (Russo & Shoemaker, 1989, pp 111-113).

I have tried to use a similar strategy in designing the thought experiments that follow. The Lawsuit Market is an attempt to reframe the positions of the litigants in a lawsuit to reverse their gain frames and loss frames. The Spinner in the Pie is a re-imagining of lawsuit probabilities. The Market Meets the Spinner is a combination of the first two. And the final experiment is an attempt to use the status quo bias as a tool to increase rather than decrease the likelihood of settlement.

§5.01 THE LAWSUIT MARKET

As all dispute resolution practitioners know, a great deal depends on whose ox is gored. Parties to a dispute have little inclination or ability to look at the case from the other person's point of view. The other side, after all, is Evil Itself, and looking at the matter from their point of view would be wrong. And besides, as we all know, my point of view is objective. I was there.

So I want to offer another approach. This one doesn't require asking parties to step into anyone else's shoes. They get to stay in their own shoes. They just have to imagine the existence of a lawsuit market.

To a plaintiff, a lawsuit is the right, under certain conditions, to take money from a defendant. To a defendant, a lawsuit is the obligation, under certain conditions, to pay money to a plaintiff. The conditions can get quite complicated. They involve whose witnesses are believed, which jurisdiction's law applies, what judge is assigned to the case and so on. And each factor has a range and probability distribution that may also be quite complicated. But if we strip all that away and look just at basic economic structure, a lawsuit involves an obligation to pay and a right to be paid.

It is then only a short step to imagine that there could be a market for lawsuits in which the roles of plaintiff and defendant could be bought and sold. The reframing I propose comes about when we ask the parties to a dispute to think of themselves as investors in this market.

We say to the plaintiff: Suppose you didn't have this lawsuit. How much would you be willing to pay to get it? In other words, we ask the plaintiff to put a value on the economic opportunity represented by his right to sue, but instead of framing it in terms of potential gain, we have him frame it as a cost.

We similarly have the defendant value the potential economic cost of the suit, but instead of thinking of it as a loss, we ask him to reframe it as a gain. We say: Suppose you weren't involved in this lawsuit. How much would someone have to pay you to endure it?

If the theorists are right about gain frames and loss frames and loss aversion and the rest, these reframed questions will generate a lower plaintiff's number and a higher defendant's number than we get when we ask the question in the customary way.

The next step is to persuade the parties that the answers they give to these questions are the valuations they themselves put on their role in their lawsuit: If you say, Mr. Plaintiff, that you would pay only x dollars to acquire your lawsuit if you didn't already have it, you are saying, are you not, that you think your lawsuit is worth x dollars.

If you say, Mr. Defendant, that you would have to be paid y dollars in order to allow yourself to be sued in this case if you weren't already in it, aren't you saying that you think this case is worth y dollars?

§5.02 THE SPINNER IN THE PIE: AN EVALUATION TOOL

Imagine you are a party in a lawsuit. Draw a circle to represent the suit. Divide the circle into a pie chart to represent different potential outcomes. If you think there is a 25 percent chance your case will be dismissed, mark off 25 percent of the circle and write zero in it. If you think there is a 35 percent chance of a recovery of $100,000, mark off 35 percent of the circle and write $100,000 in it. Keep doing this until you've marked off the whole circle into what you think are all the likely outcomes. Adjust the outcomes and the percentages until you're comfortable you've accurately captured the situation.

There is no point in cheating. The purpose of this exercise is to help you rationally determine a fair settlement value for your case. You can only hurt yourself if you exaggerate or fudge. (Robert A. Creo (2000) provides a valuable discussion of the use of pie charts in mediation of multiparty, multi-issue conflicts.)

When you're done, do the math. Multiply the percentages times the outcomes you've identified and add the results together: $(.25 \times 0 = 0) + (.35 \times 100{,}000 = 35{,}000) +$ etc.

This is a valuable exercise in itself, especially if a client and a lawyer go through it together. As suggested in §2.01(c), there is evidence that unless you are clinically depressed the number you arrive at through this process is likely to be significantly over-optimistic, but let's go on.

Once you've honestly evaluated the likely outcomes and their probabilities, the sum of those probabilities is what statisticians call an **expected value**. Let's say you came up with $75,000. That means $75,000 is your best estimate of the average recovery if you tried this case a large number of times. A classical economist would argue that after adjusting for costs and fees, you should accept any settlement offer that is better than the expected value and reject any offer that's not as good.

But it is important to understand two things about expected value:

1. Even if you did try the case 1,000 times, you might never achieve the expected outcome. This is because expected value is an average — a mathematical construct. The average American adult has one testicle. So what? As Stephen J. Gould said, "The median is not the message."
2. You aren't going to try this case 1,000 times. You are going to try it at most once.

So, while the expected value calculation tells us something about your situation, it doesn't capture the whole picture. It only tells the whole story for decision makers who are risk neutral. An insurance company that tries thousands of similar cases might be risk neutral. An individual party is not. The pie chart was effective in reducing a number of possible outcomes and probabilities down to just one number, but now we need a way to get risk back into the model.

Let's go back to the pie chart. This time imagine you have one of those spinners that came with the board games you had when you were a kid. You flick the little arrow, and it spins around and tells you how many squares to move. Put that spinner in the center of your pie chart, and now you've got an accurate model of your situation. If you are the plaintiff, you have the right to flick the spinner one time. If you're the defendant, you have the obligation to pay the plaintiff whatever he lands on.

The settlement value of this lawsuit, from the plaintiff's point of view, is the amount he would have to be paid to agree to give up his right to flick the spinner. And the settlement value from the defendant's point of view is the amount he would be willing to pay the plaintiff to get him to give up his right to spin. Note that this is not the same as expected value. Classical economists say the value of a spin is exactly the sum of the possible outcomes multiplied by their likelihoods. But classical economics doesn't take into account people's feelings about risk.

Behavioral economists, who study how people actually make economic decisions, know that people are risk averse. If you show people the wheel and spinner you just made and ask, "Which would you rather have, $75,000 or a chance to spin this wheel?" they will often look at the wheel, see that one quarter of the wheel shows a recovery of zero, and take the cash. People are risk averse. They are willing to take less than expected value in order to avoid risk.

This is less true for defendants than it is for plaintiffs — people are in general willing to take greater risk to avoid loss than they are to achieve gain — but it is still true. A defendant looking at a pie chart with a spinner in it is likely to focus on the area where he stands to lose the most, and will often agree to pay more than the expected value to avoid the risk of having to pay an even higher amount.

If what I have just said is true, the pie exercise will allow parties to get a realistic appraisal of expected value. Putting a spinner in the pie will allow them to identify a risk aversion discount off of expected value.

§5.03 THE LAWSUIT MARKET MEETS THE SPINNER IN THE PIE

We can combine the ideas from the preceding two sections for what I anticipate will be maximum effect. First, we use the pie chart to establish what each party believes to be the objective probabilities and their distribution. Then we stick the spinner in the pie to establish the party's subjective valuation of that package of probabilities.

A traditional economist would say to the plaintiff: Given that pie chart, marked with what you consider to be the objective outcome distribution pattern, assume that you will get paid whatever amount the spinner lands on after one spin. How much would someone have to pay you for the right to get the proceeds from that spin?

And the traditional economist would say to the defendant: Given that pie, marked with what you consider to be the objective outcome distribution pattern, assume that you will have to pay to the plaintiff whatever amount the spinner lands on after one spin. How much would you pay to block the spin from ever taking place?

Instead, I suggest we apply the reframing provided by the Lawsuit Market.

Now we say to the plaintiff: Suppose you didn't have this lawsuit. Instead, imagine that you are an investor in the Lawsuit Market and that you see an opportunity to invest in a lawsuit with the probabilities you have marked on this pie. How much would you pay for the right to flick that lawsuit's spinner once and collect whatever amount it lands on?

And we say to the defendant: Suppose you didn't have this lawsuit. Instead you are an investor in the Lawsuit Market, and there is a lawsuit with the probabilities you have marked here. Someone is willing to pay you a sum of money if you agree to pay the plaintiff the amount the spinner lands on. How much would you have to be paid in order to agree to do that?

§5.04 THE LAWSUIT MARKET AND THE SPINNER MEET THE STATUS QUO BIAS

There is one more step. This is designed to take advantage of regret aversion and the status quo bias. In this version we ask the parties not to think of themselves as just any investor in the Lawsuit Market but to imagine themselves as their post-settlement selves. We ask them to imagine that the case has settled. The money has been paid by the defendant and received by the plaintiff. The payment has been posted and booked. And we ask the parties to imagine un-winding the deal. Suppose the settlement under consideration is $100,000.

We say to the plaintiff: Imagine that the lawsuit is over. Suppose it settled for $100,000 with $75,000 net to you, and the money is sitting in the bank. Now, suppose this investment opportunity came up. You have the opportunity to take your $75,000 out of your bank account, put it down on the table, and spin this spinner. You have to give up your $75,000 for the privilege, but you get to keep whatever you land on. Would you do it? If not the whole $75,000, how much would you be willing to take out of the bank and bet?

And we say to the defendant: Imagine the lawsuit is over. Suppose it settled for $100,000 with $75,000 net to the plaintiff. The deal is closed, the money is paid and booked. Now this investment opportunity has come up. There is a lawsuit out there with the probabilities distributed just as you have them on this pie. Someone is willing to pay you $100,000 if you will agree to pay the plaintiff in that lawsuit what he lands on. Will you do it? If you won't do it for $100,000, how much would you have to be paid?

Having done all this, we have restated the problem in a way that reverses the effects of gain frames and loss frames; we have substituted a model that captures real attitude toward risk rather than expected value; and we have arranged to have the power of the status quo bias work in favor of settlement rather than against it. At this point I think we have a tool that will settle cases.

6

Epilogue: Gaming The System IS The System

Not long ago I arbitrated a labor case involving an attendance policy based on a point system. The company had recently implemented the new policy because, it was explained, the old policy allowed employees to "work the points." After the new system was implemented, a brief period of relatively good attendance followed, but then the employees began to work the points again. The employer became infuriated at the people who were "taking advantage" of the policy he had worked so hard to develop and fired them all.

It is easy to be amused by an employer so naïve as to think he could devise an attendance system that couldn't be gamed. It is obvious that it was only a matter of time before the employees would "solve" the new policy and begin to work the points again. We recognize that, notwithstanding all the rhetoric about how management and labor are in the same boat, it is in a manager's interest to get as much work as possible per unit of pay, and it is in a worker's interest to get as much pay as possible per unit of work. In general, we are not surprised when people adapt to circumstances and respond to incentives. We know that people and institutions evolve, and we know that each changes in response to changes in the other — they co-evolve. But for some reason there has been a failure to recognize this pattern when we see it in the history of alternative dispute resolution ("ADR").

For example, my negotiation students are dismayed to learn of the (admittedly apocryphal) businessman who sends copies of *Getting to Yes* as gifts to his potential negotiation opponents — the better to disarm them and pick their pockets with, my dear.

They should not be surprised. This is the way the world works. The parasite gets smarter, the host gets stronger. The predator gets faster, the prey figures out a way to hide. To stop evolving is to die. Lawyers and dispute resolution systems are no different; they also co-evolve. As the system changes, the lawyers working within it must also change. As the lawyers change, the system must change.

A rough historical outline of the process might look like this. Years ago lawyers ambushed one another at trial. So "new" rules of evidence were developed to allow for extensive pre-trial discovery. So lawyers buried one another in interrogatories and billed for endless depositions. So evolutionary pressure produced an arbitration system with limited discovery. So lawyers figured out ways to gum up the arbitration system — not because lawyers are in favor of gumming things up in the abstract, but because delay is usually in the interest of at least one party and because many lawyers are paid by the hour.

(Arbitration eventually got so gummed up that a lawyer recently complained to me he had a case that took several times longer to try in arbitration than it would have taken in federal court. This was because the arbitrator, who was being paid by the hour and responding to his own set of incentives, so relaxed the rules of evidence that *everything* came in. A busy federal judge with a different set of incentives would have cut those lawyers off at the knees.)

Evolutionary pressure then created mediation. There is nothing mysterious about this. Lawyers survive by making their clients happy. Clients are unhappy when they lose or when it costs so much to win that it's indistinguishable from losing. Fisher, Ury, and Patton wrote *Getting to Yes*, and it seemed to many people that we had at last reached the end of the road. But, of course, we had not. *Getting to Yes*, for all its virtues, is not the final revealed scripture. It can be gamed. And, like all other systems everywhere and always, gamed it will inevitably be.

The process has already begun. Today you can go to classes where people like Marty Latz will teach you how to use the mediation process to get more for your client, to manipulate the mediator into working for your side, to understand the mediator's goals and use those goals to move the settlement toward your end of the settlement range.

You can read a book like *Start with No* by Jim Camp, in which "America's number one negotiating coach explains why win-win is an ineffective, often disastrous strategy and how you can beat it."

Elsewhere in the field, there are lawyers involved in the process of collaborative law. They agree not to litigate and agree to withdraw from the case if litigation becomes necessary. This is an ingenious adaptation to the dispute resolution environment. It works precisely because it de-incentivizes the delay and gaming, posturing and puffing that characterize litigation practice. It also, not incidentally, takes the professional neutral out of the picture. To the collaborative lawyer, the mediator is a cost, a shrinking of the pie. From the point of view of the ADR neutral, obviously, this is dangerous blasphemy. But from the point of view of the collaborative lawyer it makes perfect sense. The collaborative lawyer's pitch is that his services are inexpensive. They are inexpensive because they do away with the unnecessary. If collaborative lawyers then bake a mediator (and mediator fees) back into the process, the collaborative process becomes less attractive.

Lawyers are in competition with each other and with other professionals for dispute resolution dollars. Like leopards and lice, baboons and bacteria, lawyers in competition for resources adapt to circumstances and respond to incentives. At the same time, the societal institutions for the resolution of disputes — the environment in which lawyers practice — are also evolving. The process and the practitioners co-evolve.

What advantages will a co-evolution model of ADR provide? I think there are three principal benefits. The co-evolution model accounts for the data better; it makes testable predictions where the older model does not; and it points in the direction of more fruitful future thinking.

If we understand that lawyers are like organisms competing for food, and we see that the food for lawyers is money, a large volume of previously unintelligible data begins to make sense. We know that when a new food source becomes available, organisms will compete for it. Different strategies will be attempted, and there is no way to tell in advance which strategy will be most successful. With this framework we can see why many retired judges who know nothing about mediation, as that term is understood by mediators, nevertheless hold themselves out as mediators. And we can see why lawyers who know nothing about mediation take their business to these retired judges. We can understand the explosive growth of the business of training and certifying mediators.

Another effect of the adoption of the co-evolution model is that much of what passes for scholarship in the field has to be rethought. The argument that ADR is or is not a Good Thing is based on a profoundly mistaken view of the way social institutions evolve. To use yet another analogy, it is like arguing that armor is good and longbows are bad or that the only real way to ride a horse is without stirrups. Longbows and stirrups are facts. It does no good to argue that they are "ungentlemanly" or that we didn't do it that way in the good old days. In precisely the same way, it is just silly to argue that, say, Baruch Bush (2005) has finally got it right and that transformative mediation is the only true mediation.

In the scientific spirit of my proposed co-evolutionary view, I will make some predictions. I predict that experienced practitioners will, if they haven't already, figure out a way to game transformative mediation and manipulate transformative mediators to achieve more favorable results for their clients. I predict that experienced collaborative law practitioners will figure out a way to game collaborative law. And I predict that a new generation of procedural innovations will evolve to counteract those changes in the practitioner population.

It is only a matter of time. Lawyers will game these systems because it is their job. Just as it is the job of a bug to evolve so it can eat bug-resistant plants. And it is the job of a plant to evolve so it is bug resistant.

The time has come to purge ADR scholarship of its cult-like character. There are important texts but no sacred texts. There is no end to the process of co-evolution. Gaming the system *is* the system.

Glossary

affirmation bias — Our tendency to agree with one another, to go along to get along. You know what I mean, right?

anchoring — Our tendency to give undue weight to some salient fact. We tend to adjust insufficiently from our anchors.

aspiration point — Your goal, the best outcome you can reasonably expect.

availability heuristic — The tendency to confuse what is most available in our memory with what is most common in the real world.

base rate — The background condition. The situation that existed before the event of interest.

BATNA — Best Alternative To a Negotiated Agreement. The best outcome you can get if the present negotiation fails.

biased punctuation of conflict — The tendency to see our attacks on our opponents as retaliatory and our opponent's attacks on us as unprovoked.

Boulwarism — Best offer first, with refusal to make any concessions thereafter.

cognitive load — The mental horsepower required to complete a task.

confirmation bias	The tendency to overweight evidence that supports what we already believe and to underweight or ignore evidence that doesn't.
consecutive unreciprocated concessions	Making two bargaining moves without an intervening move by your opponent. Bargaining against yourself.
conversational style	Those features of spoken language that are not intended to convey meaning: the length of pauses between speakers or the presence or absence of listening noises, for example.
cooperate	In game theory, to make the move that is likely to generate the most mutual gain.
counterfactual	An event that might have happened but conspicuously did not. A "what if."
defect (verb)	In game theory, to make the (uncooperative) move that is likely to generate the most individual gain.
dollar auction	A demonstration exercise in which a dollar bill is auctioned off to the highest bidder. Used to demonstrate irrational escalation of commitment, among other things.
Effective Negotiator ("EN")	An imaginary model negotiator.
endowment effect	The tendency to overvalue things that are *mine*.
expected value	The mathematical calculation of the odds times the payoff. A 50/50 chance of gaining a dollar has an expected value of 50 cents.
extremeness aversion	Our tendency to avoid the far ends of things.

fixed-pie perception The mistaken sense that my opponent wants all and only the same things I do, and therefore that our negotiation is purely distributive.

framing effect Frames are points of view, perspectives, approaches. Decision makers tend to change their mind with regard to risk tolerance depending on whether they are in a gain frame or a loss frame. Bill Ury says, "To change the game, change the frame."

fundamental attribution error Attributing a different and usually more admirable cause to my own (or my reference group's) behavior than to someone else's behavior. I was rude because I had a headache. You were rude because you're a jerk.

game theory The mathematical modeling of competition, cooperation, and strategic interaction.

groupthink A disease of decision making in groups. The tendency of certain groups to converge in their thinking, often on bad decisions.

halo effect The tendency, once we have determined that someone has some positive quality, to believe he or she has other positive qualities as well.

hindsight bias The tendency to be "insufficiently surprised." We tend, after the fact, to believe we knew it all along or that we would have seen it coming.

"You acted unwisely," I cried, "as you see By the outcome." He calmly eyed me: "When choosing the course of my action,"

said he, I had not the outcome to guide me."
– Ambrose Bierce

Homo economicus Economic man. The rational actor who will always act to maximize his individual economic benefit.

illusion of control The belief that we control events that we do not, in fact, control.

indifference point The price at which I don't care which side of a transaction I am on.

irrational escalation of commitment Continuing to put resources into a project after it stops making economic sense. Throwing good money after bad.

iterated prisoner's dilemma A prisoner's dilemma game played multiple times.

Lake Wobegon effect The almost universally held belief that we as individuals are above average.

leak An inadvertent release of information. They come in two varieties: verbal and non-verbal.

loss aversion Our tendency to give undue weight to losses. Losses loom larger than gains.

mental accounting The tendency to treat our money as if it were not fungible, as if some money should be budgeted differently than other money.

mirror and match An active listening technique in which the listener attempts to exert influence on the speaker by matching his tone, posture, and conversational style.

mutual-gains bargaining Negotiation with the goal of maximizing gains for both parties.

negotiation style An individual's overall approach to negotiation. One familiar classification of styles divides negotiators into avoiders, accommodators, compromisers, competitors, and problem solvers.

nice In game theory, a strategy is nice if it is never the first to defect.

order effect A change in choice depending on the order in which alternatives are presented.

Pareto-optimal A solution in which all the available value has been distributed and nothing is left on the table. A measure of efficiency, not fairness.

Pareto-optimal frontier The range of solutions along which neither party can do better without the other party doing worse.

partisan perception Our tendency to see the world in a way that is favorable to ourselves or people we like.

peak-end rule The tendency, when assessing the overall quality of an experience, to give excess weight to the most extreme part of the experience (the peak) and the chronologically last part (the end).

plan of concessions A map of your opening offer and the expected stages of bargaining to follow.

position effect A change in choice depending on the relative physical position of the alternatives.

possibility effect The tendency to overweight the increment that makes an event possible compared to any equivalent increment that makes the same event more or less probable. Buying one lottery ticket if we have none seems to add greater value than buying one more if we already have 20.

post-settlement settlement Continuing to bargain after we have reached an agreement. The idea is that we can now reach tradeoffs that we couldn't reach before.

preference reversal The puzzling fact that we will sometimes choose A over B and sometimes choose B over A, purely as a function of how the choice is framed.

priming The activation of a schema (a family of thoughts or feelings) by an idea or event.

Prisoner's Dilemma The classic game theory setup: Both parties will do better if they both cooperate than if they both defect, but each party will do even better if he defects and his opponent cooperates.

prominent solutions Round numbers and other settlement points to which negotiators are strongly drawn.

prospective hindsight A technique that uses the hindsight bias to improve decision making rather than harm it.

provocable In game theory, a strategy that will defect in response to some move or moves by the opponent.

pseudocertainty effect The *certainty* effect is the tendency to give more weight to the increment that makes an event certain than we give to any similar increment elsewhere in the range. The *pseudocertainty* effect is the same thing, only the overweighted increment only *seems* to make the event certain.

rapport building Words and actions used by negotiators to gain trust.

rational actor model — The assumption, in classical economics and game theory, that participants will perceive things objectively and pursue self-interest rationally.

reactive devaluation — The tendency to undervalue or reject a negotiation proposal, irrespective of its merits, because it is perceived to come from the enemy.

regret aversion — The tendency to avoid what we sense may increase the risk of regret. Given two choices with equal risk of loss, we will prefer the one that allows us to put the blame for any loss on something or someone other than ourselves.

rejection then retreat — Making a large request, having that request rejected, and then making a smaller request. Combines the psychological principle of the contrast effect with the reciprocity norm to increase the likelihood of compliance with the smaller request.

representativeness fallacy — The mistake of supposing that every member of a class will have the stereotypical features of class membership regardless of the base rate.

reservation point — The point at which a negotiator will walk away.

schema — A family of associated thoughts or feelings.

schmooze — Yiddish. Untranslatable, but "chat up" comes close.

self-serving bias — Our tendency to see ourselves in a flattering light.

similarity-attraction effect Our tendency to enjoy the company of people who are, or appear to be, similar to us.

social proof In informal logic, *argumentum ad populum*, the appeal to the people. In social psychology, the belief that the right thing to do is the thing that other people are doing.

status quo bias Our tendency to favor the existing state of affairs.

sucker's payoff In a prisoner's dilemma game, the score that goes to a cooperator (the sucker) when his opponent defects.

sunk cost fallacy The tendency to allow past costs to influence future decisions.

System 1 The unconscious, emotional, immediate, intuitive part of our mind, associated with the limbic system.

System 2 The conscious, logical part of our mind, associated with the cortical areas.

theory of mind The idea that others have thoughts and mental experiences different from our own.

timing effects A change in choice depending on the alternatives' relative position in time.

Tit for Tat ("TFT") A winning strategy for the iterated prisoner's dilemma game. TFT cooperates on the first move and, on every subsequent move, does what its opponent did on the previous move.

transformative mediation The form of mediation most focused on the personal growth of the parties rather than the resolution of a particular dipute.

winner's curse	The sinking feeling we get when our negotiation goal is achieved too easily.
zero-sum	A game in which every gain by one player means an equivalent loss by the other. A transaction that is distributive only.
zone of possible agreement ("ZOPA")	The area in which any settlement must take place. The area where parties' bargaining zones overlap.

Bibliography

Arrow, K. J., Mnookin, R. H., Ross, L., Tversky, A., and Wilson, R. B. (1995).
Barriers to conflict resolution. New York: W. W. Norton.

Axelrod, R. (1984).
The evolution of cooperation. New York: BasicBooks (HarperCollins).

Baron, J. (2000).
Thinking and deciding, 3rd ed. Cambridge, UK: Cambridge University Press.

Bazerman, M. H. and Neale, M. A. (1992).
Negotiating rationally. New York: The Free Press (Macmillan).

Belsky, G. and Gilovich, T. (1999).
Why smart people make big money mistakes — and how to correct them: Lessons from the new science of behavioral economics. New York: Fireside (Simon & Schuster).

Bohnet, I. and Zeckhauser, R. (2006).
Games of trust and betrayal. Sidebar to Lambert (2006).

Brosnan, S.F. and de Waal, F. B. M. (2003).
Monkeys reject unequal pay. *Nature, 425*: 297–299.

Burnham, T. and Phelan, J. (2000).
Mean genes: From sex to money to food — taming our primal instincts. New York: Penguin Books.

Bush, R. A. B. and Folger, J. P. (2005).
The promise of mediation: The transformative approach to conflict. San Francisco: Jossey-Bass.

Camp, J. (2002).
Start with no: The negotiating tools that the pros don't want you to know. New York: Crown Business.

Cassidy, J. (2006).
Mind games. *New Yorker* magazine, Sept. 18.

Christie, R. (1970).
The Machiavellis among us. Reprinted in Lewicki et al., 1993.

Cialdini, R. B. (1993).
Influence: The psychology of persuasion. New York: Quill (William Morrow).

Creo, R. A. (2000).
A pie chart tool to resolve multiparty, multi-issue conflicts. *Alternatives, 18*(5), p. 89. Available via Westlaw or Lexis; see directions at http://tinyurl.com/2a3n9k.

de Waal, F. B. M. (2005).
Our inner ape. New York: Penguin Group.

Ekman, P. (1992).
Telling lies: Clues to deceit in the marketplace, politics, and marriage. New York: W. W. Norton. (Original work published 1985).

Etcoff, N. (1999).
Survival of the prettiest: The science of beauty. New York: Doubleday.

Fine, C. (2006).
A mind of its own: How your brain distorts and deceives. New York: W. W. Norton.

Fischhoff, B., Lichtenstein, S., Slovic, P., Derby, S. L., and Keeney, R. L. (1981).
Acceptable risk. Cambridge, UK: Cambridge University Press.

Fisher, R. and Ury, W. (1983).
Getting to yes: Negotiating agreement without giving in. New York: Penguin Books.

Frank, R. H. (1985).
Choosing the right pond: Human behavior and the quest for status. New York: Oxford University Press.

Gilbert, D. (2006).
He who cast the first stone probably didn't. *New York Times* Op-Ed, July 24.

Gilovich, T. (1991).
How we know what isn't so: The fallibility of human reason in everyday life. New York: The Free Press (Macmillan).

Gladwell, M. (2002).
The tipping point: How little things can make a big difference. New York: Little, Brown.

Gladwell, M. (2005).
Blink: The power of thinking without thinking. New York: Little, Brown.

Goldberg, S. B., Sander, F. E. A., and Rogers, N. H. (1992).
Dispute resolution: Negotiation, mediation, and other processes, 2nd ed. Boston: Little, Brown & Company.

Groopman, J. (2007).
How doctors think. New York: Houghton Mifflin.

Hammond, J., Keeney, R., and Raiffa, H. (2001).
The hidden traps in decision making. In *Harvard Business Review* anthology.

Harvard Business Review [anthology]. (2001).
Harvard Business Review on decision making. Cambridge, MA: Harvard Business School.

Hastie, R. and Dawes, R. M. (2001).
Rational choice in an uncertain world: The psychology of judgment and decision making. Thousand Oaks, CA: Sage Publications.

Hastorf, A. and Cantril, H. (1954).
They saw a game: A case study. *Journal of Abnormal and Social Psychology, 49,* 129–134.

Henderson, M. (2006).
Why say no to free money? It's neuro-economics, stupid. *Times Online,* www.timesonline.co.uk (Oct. 7).

Hopkin, M. (2006).
Lingerie makes hagglers happy go lucky. News@Nature (doi:10.1038/news060417-1), published online April 19.

Jackson, B. and Jamieson, K. H. (2007).
Unspun: Finding facts in a world of disinformation. New York: Random House.

Janis, I. L. (1972).
Victims of groupthink: A psychological study of foreign-policy decisions and fiascoes. New York: Houghton Mifflin.

Johnson, D. D. P. (2004).
Overconfidence and war: The havoc and glory of positive illusions. Cambridge, MA: Harvard University Press.

Johnson, S. (2004).
Mind wide open: Your brain and the neuroscience of everyday life. New York: Scribner.

Kahneman, D. (2002).
Maps of bounded rationality: A perspective on intuitive judgment and choice. (Nobel Prize lecture, Dec. 8). http://nobelprize.org/nobel_prizes/economics/laureates/2002/kahnemann-lecture.pdf.

Kahneman, D. and Renshon, J. (2007).
Why hawks win. *Foreign Policy, 158* (Jan/Feb), pp. 34–38.

Kida, T. (2006).
Don't believe everything you think: The 6 basic mistakes we make in thinking. Amherst, NY: Prometheus Books.

Krivis, J. and Zadeh, M. (2006).
Hunting for deception in mediation: Winning cases by understanding body language. www.mediate.com/articles/krivis17.cfm.

Lambert, C. (2006).
The marketplace of perceptions. *Harvard Magazine, 108*(4). www.harvardmagazine.com/on-line/030640.html.

Langer, E. J. (1975).
The illusion of control. *Journal of Personality and Social Psychology, 32*(2), 311–328.

Lax, D. A. and Sebenius, J. K. (1986).
The manager as negotiator: Bargaining for cooperation and competitive gain. New York: The Free Press.

Leff, A. A. (1976).
Swindling and selling. New York: The Free Press (Macmillan).

Lewicki, R. J. et al. (eds.). (1993).
Negotiation: Readings, exercises and cases, 2nd ed., Burr Ridge, IL: R. D. Irwin.

MacKenzie, D. (2006, June 28).
Big Brother eyes make us act more honestly. *New Scientist.* www.newscientist.com/article/dn9424-big-brother-eyes-make-us-act-more-honestly.html.

Maurer, D. W. (1999 ed.).
The big con: The story of the confidence man. New York: Anchor Books (Random House). (Original work published 1940).

Medvec, V. H., Madey, S. F., and Gilovich, T. (1995).
When less is more: Counterfactual thinking and satisfaction among Olympic medalists. *Journal of Personality and Social Psychology, 69,* 603–610.

Meltsner, M. and Schrag, P. G. (1992).
Negotiating tactics for legal services lawyers. (In Goldberg, Sander and Rogers, pp. 18-23.)

Miller, G., Tybur, J. M., and Jordan, B. D. (2007).
Ovulatory cycle effects on tip earnings by lap dancers: Economic evidence for human estrus? *Evolution in Human Behavior, 28,* 6 (November), pp. 375–381. Referenced in *The Economist* (October 11), www.economist.com/science/displaystory.cfm?story_id=9942043.

Miller, J. D. (2003).
Game theory at work: How to use game theory to outthink and outmaneuver your competition. New York: McGraw-Hill.

Myers, D. G. (2002).
Intuition: Its powers and perils. New Haven, CT: Yale University Press.

Myers, D. G. (2007).
The powers and perils of intuition. *Scientific American Mind* (July).

Norman, D. A. (1989).
The design of everyday things. New York: Doubleday. (Retitled; original work published 1988).

Paulos, J. A. (1990).
Innumeracy: Mathematical illiteracy and its consequences. New York: Vintage Books (Random House). (Original work published 1988).

Piatelli-Palmarini, M. (1994).
Inevitable illusions: How mistakes of reason rule our minds. New York: John Wiley & Sons.

Plous, S. (1993).
The psychology of judgment and decision making. New York: McGraw-Hill.

Potter, S. (1947).
The theory and practice of gamesmanship: Or the art of winning games without actually cheating. New York: Henry Holt.

Poundstone, W. (1993).
Prisoner's dilemma. New York: Anchor Books. (Original published by Doubleday, 1992)

Pratkanis, A. and Shadel, D. (2005).
Weapons of fraud: A source book for fraud fighters. Washington: American Association of Retired Persons (AARP).

Pyszczynski, T. A. A., Solomon, S., and Greenberg, J. (2003).
In the wake of 9/11: The psychology of terror. Washington, DC: American Psychological Association.

Raiffa, H. (1982).
The art and science of negotiation. Cambridge, MA: The Belknap Press (Harvard University Press).

Rodell, F. (1980).
Woe unto you, lawyers! New York: Berkley Books. (Original work published 1939).

Ross, L. (1995).
Reactive devaluation in negotiation and conflict resolution. In Arrow et al., 1995.

Russo, J. E. and Schoemaker, P. J. H. (1990).
Decision traps: Ten barriers to brilliant decision-making and how to overcome them. New York: Fireside (Simon & Schuster). (Original work published 1989).

Sally, D. F. (2006).
The theory of mind. In Schneider and Honeyman (2006), p. 378.

Schelling, T. C. (1980).
The strategy of conflict. Cambridge, MA: Harvard University Press. (Original work published 1960).

Schneider, A. K. and Honeyman, C. (Eds.). (2006).
The negotiator's fieldbook: The desk reference for the experienced negotiator. Washington, DC: American Bar Association, Section of Dispute Resolution.

Schwartz, B. (2004).
The paradox of choice: Why more is less. New York: HarperCollins.

Schwartz, B. (2007).
When words decide. *Scientific American MIND* (August).

Shell, G. R. (1999).
Bargaining for advantage: Negotiation strategies for reasonable people. New York: Penguin Books.

Shermer, M. (2004).
The science of good and evil: Why people cheat, gossip, care, share, and follow the golden rule. New York: Times Books (Henry Holt).

Shestowsky, D. (2006).
Psychology and persuasion. In Schneider and Honeyman, p. 367.

Shleifer, A. (2006).
Not the whole truth: The economics of persuasion. AEA meeting presentation (Jan. 6). Downloaded from www1.fee.uva.nl/fm/PAPERS/Economics%20of%20Persuasion.pdf.

Simons, D. J. and Chabris, C. F. (1999).
Gorillas in our midst: Sustained inattentional blindness for dynamic events. *Perception, 28,* 1059-1074.

Stanovich, K. E., and West, R. F. (2000).
Individual differences in reasoning: Implications for the rationality debate. *Behavioral and Brain Sciences, 23,* 645–665.

Sutherland, S. (1994).
Irrationality: Why we don't think straight! New Brunswick: Rutgers University Press. (Original work published in Great Britain 1992).

Taleb, N. N. (2004).
Fooled by randomness: The hidden role of chance in life and in the markets, 2nd ed. New York: Thomson Texere.

Taleb, N. N. (2007).
The black swan: The impact of the highly improbable. New York: Random House.

Tannen, D. (2004).
That's not what I meant! The sociolinguistics of everyday conversation (Communication Matters II: recorded lectures based on Tannen's 1984 book of same name). Prince Frederick, MD: The Modern Scholar.

Tavris, C. and Aronson, E. (2007).
Mistakes were made (but not by me): Why we justify foolish beliefs, bad decisions, and hurtful acts. Orlando, FL: Harcourt.

Thaler, R. H. (1992).
The winner's curse: Paradoxes and anomalies of economic life. New York: Free Press.

Thompson, L. (1998).
The mind and heart of the negotiator. Upper Saddle River: Prentice Hall.

Walker, R. (2006).
Short and sweet: How limited edition candy went from novelty to glut. *New York Times Magazine,* July 7.

Wansink, B. (2006).
Mindless eating: Why we eat more than we think. New York: Bantam.

Wilson, T. D. (2002).

Strangers to ourselves: Discovering the adaptive unconscious. Cambridge, MA: Belknap Press (Harvard University Press).

Woods, V. (2005, March 18).

Pay up, you are being watched. *New Scientist.* www.newscientist.com/article.ns?id=dn7144).

Yarn, D. and Jones, G. T. (2006).

In our bones (or brains): Behavioral biology. In Schneider and Honeyman (2006).

Zaltman, G. (2003).

How customers think: Essential insights into the mind of the market. Boston: Harvard Business School Press.

Zweig, J. (2007).

Your money and your brain: How the new science of neuroeconomics can help make you rich. New York: Simon & Schuster.

Index

(References are to section numbers)

A

absolute vs. relative
determinations, 2.02(d)
accommodator (negotiation style), 2.02(a)
accounting, mental, 3.03(t)
active listening, 2.03(f)
address labels in solicitations, 3.03(a)
advertising model, 2.03(a)
African countries in UN, 3.01(a)
agreement, zone of possible, 3.02(a), 4.0
airplane parts, falling, 2.01(i)
alcoholic, 2.02(c)
aligning negotiation styles, 2.02(a)
alternative dispute resolution ("ADR")
coevolution model, 6.0
improving theoretical basis, 1.02
Always Eat As Much As You Can heuristic, 1.0, 1.03
Amazon.com shopping cart, 3.03(k)
anchoring, 3.01(a)
anecdotal vs. scientific evidence, 1.02
apartheid proposal choice, 3.03(f)
apples and oranges, trading of, 3.03(f), 4.0
approximation, cognitive errors in, 2.03
artificial numbers, 2.02(c)
Asch, Solomon, 2.03, 3.03(o)
aspiration point, 2.0
auction, feeling of loss, 2.0
authority, 2.03(c)
availability heuristic, 2.01(i)
avoider (negotiation style), 2.02(a)

B

banjolele, 3.03(j)
bank examiner scam, 2.03(c)
bank loan, offer variations, 3.03(e)
bank teller, 2.01(k)
bar drinks, taking turns, 3.03(a)
bargaining confounds, 3.03
barge salvage choices, 3.03(h)
base rates, 2.01(b)
BATNA
focusing on, 2.0

Level One agreement, 4.0
beer, cold, 3.03(d)
belief in a just world, 2.01(g)
Berra, Yogi, 2.03(e)
biased punctuation of conflict, 3.03(r)
blinking, 2.03(e)
Boulware, Lemuel Ricketts, 3.03(e)
Boulwarism, 3.03(e)
bread machine, 3.03(d)
briefcase purchase, 2.02(d)
Brosnan, Sara, 1.02
Buddha, 2.0
Bush, Baruch, 6.0

C

Cadillac test drive, 3.03(k)
Camp, Jim, 6.0
candy, limited edition, 3.03(j)
cards, testing rule for, 3.03(l)
case evaluation, factors 2.01(n)
case, market value of, 3.04
Catholic church, devil's advocate in, 3.03(o)
certainty effect, 3.03(w)
cheater detection, 3.03(l)
cheeseburgers in park, 3.03(b)
Chesterfield, Lord, 2.03(b), 2.03(f)
child custody, 3.03(g)
choices, 3.03(e)
  barge salvage, 3.03(h)
  child custody awards, 3.03(g)
  excessive number of, 3.03(f)
  informational value, 3.03(e), 3.03(f)
  spring break, 3.03(g)
Christie, Richard, 2.02(a)
Cialdini, Robert, 2.02(c), 3.04
coach, favoring high-paid players, 3.03(p)
cocaine, 3.03(j)
coevolution
  of ADR models and gambits, 6.0
  of predator and prey, 3.03(e)
coffee club, 2.02
cognitive load, 2.03(e)
coin flip experiment, 3.03(h)
Coke and raffle ticket, 3.03(a)
colonoscopy discomfort, 4.02
commitment and consistency, 3.03(k)
commitment, re-evaluation of, 2.0
commode auction, 2.0
comparator, effect on attitude, 4.01
competitor (negotiation style), 2.02(a)
compromiser (negotiation style), 2.02(a)
concession
  consecutive unreciprocated, 3.02
  making the last, 4.02
  progressive reduction, 3.03(i)
  reciprocal, 3.01(b), 3.03(a)
  timing of, 3.03(i)
confirmation bias, 3.03(l)
conflict, biased punctuation of, 3.03(r)
confounding variables (confounds), 3.03
conjunction fallacy, 2.01(k)
consecutive unreciprocated concessions, 3.02
consistency trap, 3.03(k)
contrast effect, 2.02(d)
conversational style, 3.03(s)

cookie, search for hidden, 3.03(m)
cooperate, in game theory, 3.03(b)
cooperative vs. competitive style, 2.02(a)
couch purchase, 2.02(d)
counterfactuals, 4.01
credit vs. savings account, 3.03(t)
credit surcharge vs. cash discount, 3.03(t)
criminal charges, effect of order, 3.01(a)
cultural expectations in bargaining, 3.01(b)

D

dam, project momentum, 3.03(p)
deal, taking vs. losing day's effort, 3.03(p)
decisions-already-made pile, 3.03(k)
defect, in game theory, 3.03(b)
defendant, reframing, 5.01–5.04
delay in responding, as signal, 3.03(i)
dermatologist, 3.03(u)
desk drawer junk, 2.01(e)
devil's advocate vs. groupthink, 3.03(o)
de Waal, Frans, 1.02
diagnosis momentum, 3.03(m)
dice, 2.01(f)
dinner-or-show decision, 3.03(t)
directional tendency, 2.03
discounting of future payoff or sacrifice, 3.03(u)
distortions, obstruction to settlement, 4.03
diversity, to counteract groupthink, 3.03(o)
dollar auction, 3.03(q)
dollars, fungible, 3.03(d), 3.03(t)
drawing-class teacher 2.03(f)
DVD player, 2.01(d)

E

elders as authorities, 2.03(c)
elephants, 1.0
elevated blood count, 3.03(m)
elevator, time to walk to, 3.03(x)
elimination of risk, 3.03(v)
Emmylou, what's best for, 3.03(k)
endowment effect, 2.01(e)
envious, in game theory, 3.03(b)
escalation of commitment, irrational, 3.03(q)
evolutionary psychology (and critics of), 1.02
exaggerations, obstruction to settlement, 4.03
expected value, 5.02
extremeness aversion, 3.03(v)
eye shifting, 2.03(e)

F

face lift, 2.03(a)
fairness 1.01
faking
- of advantageous traits, 2.03(a)
- of authority, 2.03(c)

farfelator, 2.02(b)
fear, cognitive effects on, 2.01(i)
fighting, symbolic vs. merciless, 2.03(b)
Fine, Cordelia, 2.01(d), 3.03(g), 3.03(x)
finger pressure, estimating, 3.03(r)
first impression, 2.03
first offer, options in responding to, 3.02
Fischhoff, Baruch, 5.0

Fisher, Roger, 2.0, 6.0
fixed-pie perception, 3.03(f)
flight insurance, 2.01(k)
flight missed, 4.01
flight recorder, 2.03(c)
flinching as tactic, 3.02(b)
fondling or manipulating, 2.03(e)
food, cognitive influence of, 2.03(d)
football infractions, 3.03(n)
foot-leg motion, rocking, 2.03(e)
framing
  certain loss vs. insurance, 3.03(h)
  mortality rate vs. survival rate, 3.03(h)
  radiation therapy vs. surgery, 3.03(h)
framing effect, 3.03(h)
full vs. discounted valuation, 3.03(u)
fundamental attribution error, 2.01(h)
furniture moving, 2.01(l)

G

gains, segregation of, 3.03(u)
gallery, 3.01(a)
game theory, 3.03(b)
gamesmanship, 2.02
gaming the ADR system, 6.0
general proposition, agreeing to, 2.03(d)
generosity, being watched, 2.02
"Gift of the Magi" scenario, 4.03
Gilbert, Daniel, 3.03(r)
gloating, 4.04
golf balls, 2.01(e)
good-cop / bad-cop, 2.02(d)
Gould, Stephen J., 5.02
Groopman, Jerome, 3.03(k)
groupthink, 3.03(o)

H

halo effect, 2.03
hand gesturing, 2.03(e)
happiness, 2.0
happy-unhappy, question framing, 3.03(g)
Hastie, Reid, 3.01(a)
hawkishness, biases reinforcing, 4.05
health club member, 3.03(p)
heart, removal of fluid around, 3.03(k)
Heineken beer, 3.03(d)
helpfulness, priming for, 3.03(x)
herd instincts, 3.03(o)
heuristics defined, 1.0
hindsight bias, 5.0
hiring manager favoring employee 3.03(p)
Hockenberry, John, 2.0
Hollywood negotiation, 3.03(i)
Holmes, Justice O. W., 2.01(e)
Homo economicus theory, 1.01
horse race, 2.01(f)
horse stall, mucking out, 2.01(d)
housework contribution, 2.01(i)
hypothetical questions, use of, 4.03

I

ice cream serving size, 2.02(d)
illusion of control, 2.01(f)
image manipulation, 2.02
indifference, in economics, 3.03(f)
indifference point defined, 2.01(e)
information gathered in schmoozing, 2.03(d)
insurance premium, 3.03(h)
intelligence, priming for, 3.03(x)

investment decision, as influenced by
  regret aversion, 2.01(m)
  status quo bias, 2.01(l)
Iraq war, sunk costs of, 3.03(p)

J

jade figure, 3.01(a)
jam choices, 3.03(f)
jury award range, 3.01(a)
justification, random, 2.02(c)

K

Kahneman, Daniel, 1.01, 3.03(h), 4.05
Keillor, Garrison, 2.01(a)
Kida, Thomas, 2.01(a)
Kismet (robot), 2.02
Krivis, Jeffrey, 2.03(e)

L

Lake Wobegon effect, 2.01(a)
Langer, Ellen, 2.02(c)
lateness, reasons for, 2.01(h)
laughing with audience, 3.03(o)
lawsuit market, 5.01–5.04
leaks, 2.03(e)
leg, value of, 3.03(o)
Level One/Two/Three agreements, 4.0, 4.04
leverage, actual and perceived, 2.02
leverage, signalling of, 3.03(i)
librarian vs. salesman, 2.01(b)
liking, 2.03(a)
limited-time offer, 3.03(j)
Linda story, 2.01(k)
line length, guessing of, 3.03(o)
listening, 2.03(e)
listening conspicuously, 2.03(f)
Loewenstein, George, 1.01
log-roll, 4.03
loss aversion and framing effects, 3.03(h)
losses, integration of, 3.03(u)
lottery
  illusion of control, 2.01(f)
  probability, 2.01(j)

M

Mach score, 2.02(a)
Machiavelli, Niccolo, 2.02(a)
mandolin, 3.03(j)
map of concessions, 2.02(b)
marginal utility, diminishing, 3.03(u)
mating schema, priming of, 3.03(x)
meaning of life, 2.0
mediation, transformative, 3.03(x)
mediator
  training of, 6.0
  weapons of, 3.04
Meltsner & Schrag, 2.02(d)
mental accounting, 3.03(t)
mercy, bargainer's plea for, 4.04
Mideast conflict, 3.03(r)
midpoint as prominent solution, 3.02(a)
Mierding, Nina, 3.01(b)
military group size, 2.01(i)
mind, theory of, 3.03(m)
mirror-and-match tactic, 2.03(b)
mismatched negotiation styles, 2.02(a)
modus ponens vs. *modus tollens*, 3.03(l)
money pump, 3.03(h)
monkey justice, 1.02
mortality vs. survival rate, 3.03(h)
Mullainathan, Sendhil, 3.03(e)

multiplying numbers, 2.03
Mutt and Jeff tactic, 2.02(d)
mutual gains bargaining, 3.03(f)

N

negatively worded statements, 2.03(e)
negotiating neighborhood, 3.01(a)
negotiation style, 2.02(a)
negotiation team, size of, 3.03(o)
neoteny, 2.03(a)
nice, in game theory, 3.03(b)
Nietzsche, Friedrich, 3.03(k)
nonfluencies, 2.03(e)
norm, oneself as representing, 2.01(d)
Norman, Donald, 2.01(d)
now, bias in favor of, 3.03(u)
nuclear standoff, recalling dialog about, 3.03(r)
number series, rule for, 3.03(m)

O

Olympic medals, 4.01
opening offer, 2.02(b)
opponent, comfort vs. discomfort, 2.02
order effect, 3.03(v)
oriental rug tryout, 3.03(k)
overconfidence, 2.01(c)
  real vs. feigned, 2.01(c)
  test for 2.01(c)
overweighting of certainty, 3.03(v)
oxytocin, effect on trust, 3.03(h)

P

packaging effects, 3.03(d)
panty hose, consumer ratings of, 3.03(v)
Pareto, Vilfredo, 4.0
Pareto efficiency, 4.03
Pareto-optimal distribution, 4.0
Pareto-optimal frontier, 4.0
partisan perception, 3.03(n)
Paulos, John Allen, 2.01(j)
pauses, 2.03(e)
payoff matrix, in game theory, 3.03(b)
peak-end rule, 4.02
pharmaceutical sales rep, 2.03(a)
Piatelli-Palmarini, Massimo, 2.01(j), 3.03(v)
plaintiff, reframing, 5.01–5.04
plan of concessions, 2.02(b)
point of view, accommodating, 3.03(k)
pollution, 3.03(b)
position effect, 3.03(v)
positive test strategy, 3.03(g)
positivity bias, 3.03(l)
possibility effect, 3.03(w)
post-settlement settlement, 4.03
potatoes, price of, 3.03(f)
Potter, Stephen, 2.02
potrzebie, 3.03(j)
preference reversals, 3.03(h)
pregnancy, reason for, 2.01(g)
priming, 3.03(x)
Prisoner's Dilemma, 2.02(a), 3.03(b)
probability, 2.01(j)
prominent solution, 2.02(b)
prospective hindsight, 5.0
provocable, in game theory, 3.03(b)
pseudocertainty effect, 3.03(v)
pupil dilation, 2.03(e)
Pyszczynski, Tom, 3.03(x)

Q

question framing, 3.03(g)

R

radiation therapy vs. surgery, 3.03(h)
Raiffa, Howard, 4.03
reactive devaluation, 3.03(f)
reasonable adult role 2.01(n)
reasons, real and specious, 2.02(c)
recasting 2.01(n), 3.03(k)
reciprocity, 3.03(a), 3.03(c)
recission of sales agreements, 3.03(e)
regret aversion, 2.01(m)
rejection then retreat, 3.03(c)
relationship between parties, 3.02
relative determinations, 2.02(d)
repulsive solution, 2.02(b)
representativeness fallacy, 2.01(b)
reservation point, defined, 2.0
risk, elimination of, 3.03(v)
robot eyes, 2.02
Rodell, Fred, 2.01(l)
round number, 2.02(b)
rudeness, priming for, 3.03(x)

S

safety sign and billboard, 3.03(k)
salesman, feigning common interest, 2.03(b)
salesman vs. librarian, 2.01(b)
Samuelson and Zeckhauser, 2.01(l)
scarcity, 3.03(j)
Schelling, Thomas, 2.0, 2.02(b)
schemas, 3.03(x)
schmooze (rapport building), 2.03
Schwartz, Barry, 3.03(f)
self-serving bias, 2.01(d)
settlement valuation, risk aversion in, 5.02–5.04
sex cue, priming, 3.03(x)
shark, getting eaten by, 2.01(i)
Shell, G. Richard, 2.02(a), 3.03(f)
shoe lifts, 2.03(a)
similarity-attraction effect, 2.03(b)
simple, in game theory, 3.03(b)
Sinclair, Upton, 3.03(m)
skin cancer vs. blackheads, 3.03(u)
sleeping without blanket, 2.0
smiling stranger, 2.03(b)
smoking while praying, 2.02(d)
social proof, 3.03(o)
song, tapping out rhythm, 3.03(m)
spacing of pleasure or pain, 3.03(u)
speaking pitch, 2.03(e)
speech errors, 2.03(e)
spinner in the pie, for evaluation, 5.02–5.04
spinner wheel, rigged, 3.01(a)
spring break, 3.03(g)
stakes vs. maintaining relationships, 3.02
status quo bias, 2.01(l), 5.04
stickiness of number with a story, 2.02(c)
storytelling, in conjunction fallacy, 2.01(k)
stranger, whether to trust, 2.03(b)
Strategic Arms Limitation Talks, 3.03(f)
student evaluation of professor, 2.03
style of negotiation, 2.02(a)
sucker's payoff, in game theory, 3.03(b)
sunk cost fallacy, 3.03(p)

swans, white and black, 3.03(l)
Syntocinon®, effect on trust, 3.03(h)
system, gaming of, 6.0

T

table circling, 2.02(a)
taking ownership of agreements, 3.03(e)
Taleb, Nassim Nicholas, 2.01(j)
Talmud, 2.0
Tannen, Deborah, 3.03(s)
tax subsidies, voting for, 3.03(k)
taxonomy of negotiations, 3.02
tennis
 alcoholic player, 2.02(c)
 calling shots, 3.03(n)
10,000th-customer prize, 4.01
Thaler, Richard, 2.01(b), 3.03(u)
theory of mind, 3.03(m)
Thomas-Kilman Instrument (TKI), 2.02(a)
Thompson, Leigh, 3.03(x), 4.0
threat vs. warning, 3.03(j)
tie shopping, 2.03(b)
timing effects, 3.03(u)
Tit for Tat ("TFT") program, 3.03(b)
tofu factory, 3.03(b)
training package promises, 3.02
transformative mediation, 3.03(x)
trial, road to (status quo bias), 2.01(l)
tribe
 following actions of, 3.03(o)
 member of, 2.03(b)
turn-taking in conversation, 3.03(s)
Tversky, Amos, 3.03(h)

U

ultimatum game, 1.01
underage drinking, testing for, 3.03(l)
unreciprocated consecutive concessions, 3.02
Ury, William, 2.0, 3.03(k), 6.0
used car sales, 3.03(j)
utility maximization theory, 1.01

V

vacuum cleaner sales contracts, 3.03(e)
validating, 2.03(f)
value, expected, 5.02
values, accommodating, 3.03(k)
Vietnam war, sunk costs of, 3.03(p)
viruses and vaccines, 3.03(v)
vomiting from placebo, 2.03(c)

W

war, cognitive biases promoting, 4.05